University of East Anglia

NON-FICTION

MA Creative Writing
Anthologies 2014

UEA NON-FICTION ANTHOLOGY 2014

First published by Egg Box Publishing 2014

International ©2014 retained by individual authors

This book is sold subject to the condition that it shall not, by way of trade or otherwise, be lent, resold, hired out, stored in a retrieval system, or otherwise circulated without the publisher's prior consent in any form of binding or cover other than that in which it is published and without a similar condition including this condition being imposed on
the subsequent purchaser.

A CIP record for this book is available from
the British Library.

UEA NON-FICTION ANTHOLOGY 2014
is typeset in Caslon. Titles are set in Din condensed, with subtitles in Gotham.

Printed and bound in the UK by Imprint Digital.

Designed and typeset by Sean Purdy.

Proofread by Sarah Gooderson.

Distributed by Central Books.

ISBN: 9780957661189

ACKNOWLEDGEMENTS

Thanks are due to the School of Literature, Drama and Creative Writing at UEA in partnership with Egg Box Publishing for making this anthology possible.

We'd also like to thank the following people:

Trezza Azzopardi, Amit Chaudhuri, Giles Foden, Sarah Gooderson, Lavinia Greenlaw, Rachel Hore, Kathryn Hughes, Daniel Leeson, James Lasdun, Michael Lengsfield, Frances Leviston, Jean McNeil, Natalie Mitchell, Beatrice Poubeau, Sophie Robinson, Helen Smith, Henry Sutton, Val Taylor, Steve Waters, Peter Womack and Toby Young.

Nathan Hamilton at Egg Box Publishing and Sean Purdy.

Editorial team:

Michelle Brown
Susan K Burton
Niall Cunniffe
John Dennehy
Hannah Coneys
Affly Johnson
Ella Micheler
Lauren Razavi
Anealla Safdar
Rebecca White

CONTENTS

Foreword
Philip Gwyn Jones—**07**

Introduction
Kathryn Hughes—**09**

Contributors
Helen de Borchgrave—**13**

Susan K Burton—**19**

Lisa Climie—**25**

Hannah Coneys—**31**

Catherine Conroy—**37**

John Dennehy—**43**

Deborah Jay—**49**

Gwenllian Jones—**55**

Leslene Kwame—**61**

Amy McTighe—**67**

Peter Noble—**73**
Charlotte Peacock—**79**

Lauren Razavi—**85**

Bridget Read—**91**

Suzanna Rose—**97**

Phyllida Scrivens—**103**

FOREWORD

Philip Gwyn Jones

Economically and geopolitically, Britain's role on the world stage gets smaller and smaller with each passing year, but conversely, and perhaps even perplexingly, our cultural clout grows and grows. Nowhere is this more obvious than in our literature, which remains disproportionately represented, in translation, in all the other countries of the world, and so often stands for Britishness (or its constituent national parts) before all else. In literature, we lead. And in recent times, we have led the world in our rewriting – in tandem with our North American cousins, it must be acknowledged – of the rules of how non-fiction can be written.

Not so long ago, a biography had to begin in the cradle and end in the grave, a travel book had to take in famous sights or distant horizons and report back as if at the Royal Geographical Society lectern, a history book had to strain to avoid anything that smelt of the theatrical or the emotive, a science book had to import the dusty patina of the laboratory intact and uncleansed, and an art book had to progress through the galleries of time and style in an orderly, hushed fashion. And none was permitted to yoke together disparate matter or disparate structural forms in the one volume. Now, non-fiction writers are entirely free to take the techniques and tricks of their colleagues in the world of fiction and deploy them in their art, to hybridise to their hearts' content, and even to look to other media for ideas about how best to communicate their passions, arguments and anxieties. That many of the most brilliant up-and-coming creative talents in this country still understand that The Book offers perhaps more space

PHILIP GWYN JONES

and more freedom and yet also requires more discipline than all other expressive and argumentative art forms is a testament to its genius, its durability, its malleability and to the great British gift for reinvention.

In recent times, readers worldwide have thrilled to the new environmental writing of Caspar Henderson, Mark Lynas and Esther Woolfson; the new science writing of Olivia Judson, Alex Bellos and Marcos du Sautoy; the new criticism of Daniel Swift, Edmund Gordon or Christopher Turner; the new political writing of David Runciman, George Monbiot or Owen Jones; the new biography of Sarah Bakewell, Rebecca Mead or Olivia Laing; the new psychoanalytical writing of Stephen Grosz or Josh Cohen; the new psychological memoir of Andrea Gillies, Gwyneth Lewis and Joanne Limburg. I could witter on for pages with such a litany of creativity; there is so much that thrills in recent creative non-fiction from writers resident in the UK. And here now is the next wave, coming out of UEA's renowned course.

Remember: all the best stories are true.

Philip Gwyn Jones
Editor-at-large, Scribe UK

INTRODUCTION

Kathryn Hughes

THIS YEAR'S NON-FICTION WRITERS HAVE PROVED THEMSELVES ENTHUSIASTIC TRAVELLERS IN BOTH TIME AND SPACE. In this anthology you'll find pieces set in Japan, Poland and Egypt together with explorations of the 18th-century art world, 19th-century boarding schools and battle tactics from the 1940s. Even the occasional stay-at-home author takes flight into a parallel universe of deep dreaming.

The range of work on show here reflects the flexibility and capaciousness of our Creative Non-Fiction programme. Students come to write memoir, biography, travel odysseys, war reportage, sport or food writing and, most excitingly, work that refuses to fit any category at all. You never quite know what you're going to get and that, really, is the fun and beauty of it all.

Starting as far away from Norwich as you can possibly get, Susan K Burton explores the Japanese phenomenon of 'rent a vicar', by which mild-looking British men make a living by dressing up in clerical garb and 'marrying' young local couples. Amazingly, it's consensual, legal and very big business. From there we spin away to Ecuador where John Dennehy, a young man in voluntary exile from Bush-era America, finds himself about to get deported from the new, rebellious country he has come to love.

Lauren Razavi also encounters the impact of violent upheaval. An inveterate traveller, she fetches up in Egypt during the Arab Spring and finds herself caught up in an interminable wait for a train that seems to bear all the metaphorical weight of the country's political situation. Amy McTighe tells the story of one Kurdish family fleeing from Saddam's hateful chemical attacks in 1988. Meanwhile, Helen de Borchgrave makes a journey to Solidarity-era Poland, determined not simply to mend the beautiful artwork that has been damaged under communism, but to find the courage to leave her violent marriage.

The mid-twentieth century continues to be the new 'hot spot' for historians and biographers. Phyllida Scrivens gives us a gripping story of courage and friendship set in 1944 on a dank bridge somewhere between Belgium and Holland. Suzanna Rose reconstructs the early womanhood of her mother, a young codebreaker at Bletchley Park. In both cases these are stories that might have disappeared into the unrecorded past, and it is consoling to know that such excellent writers are engaged in the hard graft of narrative rescue.

Another trio of our writers have pushed further back into history, to tell stories of people far removed from them in time and place. Deborah Jay brings us the strange tale of Giovanni Battista Lusieri, the Italian artist who enabled Lord Elgin to walk off with the marbles from the Acropolis. Leslene Kwame presents the story of Dr Edward Atkinson, an apparently exemplary English gentleman who went out to Antarctica with Scott but whose identity is more tangled than anyone could possibly have guessed. Charlotte Peacock goes in pursuit of Nan Shepherd, the author of *The Living Mountain*, that classic love song to the Cairngorms. Does it matter, Peacock asks, that she herself has never cared for even the smallest hills?

Four memoirists pull us into the heart of their lives. Catherine Conroy warns against buying a run-down house when you're grieving, while Peter Noble becomes 12 again, a smashed up schoolboy who may never learn to walk or think straight. Gwenllian Jones finds traces of her mother – which is to say traces of herself – in one of Manet's most famours portraits, while Lisa Climie pegs her past to the repeated seasons. Bridget Read reads her own dreams with an ingenious wit that might stump Freud. What, you wonder, would the good doctor have made of her dog suddenly sprouting Michael Jackson's hair?

Finally, we have Hannah Coneys with her sad, sweaty and enthralling account of a tragedy that occurred during the Tour de France of 1967. Not only is all human life here, but UEA's non-

INTRODUCTION

fiction writers are making certain that it is told in ways that make it new and, in the best ways, strange.

Kathryn Hughes
Director of the MA in Biography and Creative Non-Fiction

HELEN DE BORCHGRAVE
To Poland 1984 – Finding Freedom

The opening of the first chapter of a transforming visit to Poland in March 1984

I WAS LUCKY AT HEATHROW. Piling my suitcase and bulging bags onto the scales, I looked anxiously at the counter clerk as the indicator bounced into overweight. He smiled kindly.

'Last week's plane to Warsaw had difficulty taking off,' he joked, as he replaced an errant orange, and handed back my holdall. Others were not as fortunate. In the departure lounge reserved for our flight, a bird-like woman with a strong Polish accent said tearfully, 'They charged me thirty pounds for a sack of tinned food I am taking to my mother-in-law. She is dying.'

Other women also carried coats. Though March had come, several months would pass before memories of the numbing cold of this particular winter faded. It was 1984. Steely Party workers, with pale blue, lifeless eyes, were dressed in new clothes. Heavily made up, the women felt superior: they were going home to dominate. These dull reminders of communist officialdom stood out among the more human, ordinary people – relatives, friends and those with a sense of social responsibility, who were bringing crumbs of comfort and vital supplies in their overweight luggage.

Two things drew me to Poland – Lady Salisbury's *Medical Aid for Poland* fund and a Christmas letter from Gdansk. My admiration for the former's commitment to raising money and taking trucks to Poland was galvanised by the difficulties lightly described

TO POLAND 1984 – FINDING FREEDOM

by Basia, a student of English who had been allowed out for the summer holidays to look after our two sons eight years earlier. She mentioned intense cold, curfews, shortages. Poland was a lifestyle away from the padded comfort of London. Anger spurred me into action. Travelling to Poland seemed the natural thing to do. Friends filled my suitcase; my husband let me go. Before I knew it, I was transported to a truly foreign land and vastly different cities: Gdansk, Krakow, Warsaw.

Andre Dzierzynski, a Polish artist and BBC World Service contributor, said to me before I left, 'Going to Poland is a healing experience.' A man of devout faith, whose family lost everything after World War II, as well as twenty-eight of its members, he understood deeper realities and the necessity for mercy, justice and truth.

Beneath the prevailing dread, unanswered questions hovered like wraiths in the artificial air during that two-hour flight. What state was Poland in now, eight months after the repeal of Martial Law? Beside me sat a tall, handsome woman, a genetic specialist, who also drove a lorry regularly to her homeland with medical supplies for children. Mrs Ferguson was flying to Warsaw to inspect an orphanage. She carried serum, and a teddy bear. The diet in Poland was so poor that many children suffered from rickets and anaemia and there were no vitamins or minerals to supplement. I thought of the few oranges and lemons in my bag.

'Every bit helps,' she said. I could feel the pain behind her words.

'I was one of the lucky ones that survived. Did you know eighteen percent of the population died in the war?' I did not.

'My father was one of the million or two Poles sent to Siberian labour camps in 1940. When Stalin joined the Allies after Hitler invaded Russia, he granted an amnesty. The deportees were released, and my father joined General Anders's army and was one of the lucky ones at Tobruk and Monte Cassino.'

'Why was an amnesty necessary?'

'Stalin had to justify himself for non-existent crimes.' She looked round cautiously, then leaning closer, whispered, 'Don't forget, communism as practised is based on lies and deceit. It is utterly corrupt, utterly cruel.' This intelligent, caring woman – in stark contrast to some of those around us – explained something of the mentality of this subjugated state. She spoke calmly and cautiously, for we were conscious of other ears. Later, I wished I had listened more carefully. In my privileged world, freedom was an inherent part of life; or so I thought then. I did not realise, sitting in that plane, how Poland would change me. I was nearly forty and nearly blind. In Poland, my eyes began to open.

As the plane descended, the grey concrete blocks of post-war Warsaw jutted out of the plain like rectangular rocks. The squat square airport building loomed nearer, taking on the character of a cage. The plane touched down on the tyre-scorched tarmac, and slowly taxied towards the airport terminal crowned with huge letters: WARSZAWA. Young soldiers, clad in pre-war khaki greatcoats and top boots, stood at the foot of the steps gripping rifles, as the passengers alighted, laden like tramps with their fat plastic bags. Some held bunches of flowers. Armed police escorted us from the plane. The first queue on Polish soil began, inevitably, with passport control. It took several minutes for papers to be scrutinised, a blacklist checked, the passport stamped and handed back. A uniformed woman noted down my hard currency, wedding ring and pearl earrings.

Sweating palms and tightening solar plexus revealed the rising tension as we waited for the luggage to go through, then the relief as my suitcase was marked with chalk, as they were in England before automation. Underneath the piles of tights and tea, soap, coffee, chocolate, paper and vitamins were books I had been given by Keston College to smuggle in to publishers in Krakow. It was pitifully little for a nation that lacked everything, yet each gift had been given to me in London; each was a sign that someone in the West cared. This, I was to discover, was what mattered most in this seemingly forgotten land.

I huddled inside my fur coat and took stock. Basia's letter had arrived barely a month earlier. Reading between the lines, it struck me that this gentle girl, a gifted English teacher, had survived that winter when the temperature dropped to minus thirty degrees without boots. Boots, if they were obtainable, cost a month's salary. Two university friends had accompanied Basia to England in 1976 – Ewa worked for friends of ours, and Ela pulled pints in a Norfolk pub. Good-natured, hardworking and uncomplaining, Basia had soon charmed us with her ready wit and lively descriptions of life back home. Life had deteriorated sharply since those days when you could at least buy chocolates. Her generation had seen the economy crumble, Solidarity rise, freedom tasted... then Martial Law imposed. Dreams were shattered as Solidarity leaders were interned, innocent people battered or killed, curfew imposed, and tenuous threads with the outside world cut.

A glass wall separated new arrivals from the captive crowd. A sea of faces bobbed about the other side. Then one I recognised swam into view – slim, dark, and pretty, she waved boisterously. I hitched the overcoats over my arm, lifted my bags and staggered through the narrow gate. As it clicked behind me, I entered Poland. Basia hugged me close – East and West embraced.

'Quickly, Helen, we must take a taxi to the Central Station. There is only one Express train to Gdansk at this time. I have reserved us seats. Thank God you were not delayed.' She picked up my suitcase and led me through the thicket of humanity, out of the building and into a taxi. As I peeled off layers of clothing, she giggled.

'This coat is for Daniel. I hope it fits.'

Her eyes widened and tears began to fill them as she slowly took the coat, felt the cloth and began to stroke it, as if she was imagining her husband inside it, feeling warm. We reached the centre of the city, with few cars on its wide boulevards.

'That monstrosity is the Palace of Culture.' With pursed lips, Basia pointed to a distorted derivation of pre-war New York.

'Stalin gave that to the Poles as a gift. We are lumbered with this landmark in the centre of our capital to remind us who is boss.' Basia sighed. It was, I discovered later, an understated sigh. The station was nearby and, like everything else in post-war Warsaw, rebuilt. The platforms were underground. As we sat waiting on a hard wooden bench, I began to absorb the atmosphere. Saul Bellow's Herzog was right: Poland can be drab and grey. This country, lying between Germany and Russia, had been a killing ground of two world wars, and now its people lived in poverty despite its rich agricultural land and material resources. The systematic exploitation by the Party continued unabated.

The first-class compartment of the express train was spacious, clean and comfortable. Within half an hour it was no longer possible to see the wasting, crumbling buildings that littered the skyline; the pock-marked roads; the dirt and decay which spoke clearly of a people without incentive or hope. When darkness enveloped the sky, an old steam engine hissed and roared by, gushing white smoke upwards. Glimpses of a fiery furnace being stoked up evoked childhood memories. Poland lagged thirty years behind us. I took in Basia's well-cut tweed suit. Survivors learned to look well turned out even when there was nothing to buy in the shops. During the four-hour train journey I plied her with questions, and she answered patiently, with the shade of a smile hovering around the corners of her mouth. She had stayed with us in Chelsea; she was painfully aware how different the world she lived in was. To counteract the constant feeling of humiliation, Poles are extraordinarily generous and kind.

'How much do you earn as an English teacher? How much was the train ticket? Can't you buy shoes?' Neutral questions; no political talk in this public place.

With quiet courtesy, Basia explained. The monthly salary of a teacher of English at the Medical Academy was about £60, the train ticket for two was £20. There were constant shortages, mainly due to incompetent distribution. If televisions, washing machines, soap, loo paper or anything else arrived in a shop, there was an instant queue. Demand was constant; supply intermittent. Goods with a built-in obsolescence in the West were investments, for inflation, officially at 30%, was nearer 90%.

The catalogue of statistics was depressing – how do you live, day after day, under this straitjacket of deprivation? I met many Poles during my stay, from various walks of life. In contrast to Party members, each one seemed filled with courage, patient endurance and inner strength.

In Gdansk, Basia took me to the hostel for scientists, university lecturers, engineers and other intelligentsia, where Ewa and her husband Andrew lived. They had procured me a guest room there for five nights. Wooden sledges made a mountain in the outer hall, prams and pushchairs in the inner. The hostel was eight years old. It had not worn well. Cracks seared crooked paths along the walls, paint peeled, wafer-thin curtains clung limply to plastic rails. Ten families shared a kitchen. Ewa and Andrew had to stow everything away neatly if they wanted space to move around in their tiny bedsit where, in Polish fashion, the bed converted to a sofa. The room was warm and snug. One cost few Poles forego is heating. Sub-zero temperatures may hover through the winter, sleet may follow snow, but inside, especially in State-owned buildings, the temperature was high.

'I teach English to medical students,' explained Ewa as we sat round a little table eating cold meat and potato salad.

'The text books I use are written and published in Poland, but sometimes they are not available when the academic year starts. The students have to share copies and cannot take them home. Like library books, they tend to get "lost". I love teaching. Time spent with colleagues, though, can be tiring. I can't discuss my feelings, as Party members infiltrate, usually among the administrators.' Ewa apologised for not providing a more substantial meal.

'It's a pity. We Poles love our food.'

Helen de Borchgrave is a picture restorer, art critic and author of *A Journey into Christian Art* (Lion, 1999). A visit to Poland in 1984 enabled her to escape a violent husband. Each spring from 1985 to 1987 she restored pictures in Krakow's Wawel Castle State Museum while fighting a contested divorce.

SUSAN K BURTON
RENT A VICAR

The role of the white guy in Japanese wedding ceremonies

THE DOORS AT THE BACK OF THE CHAPEL SWING OPEN TO REVEAL THE COUPLE, the groom in a white morning suit, the bride in strapless white satin with rows of frills down the skirt. Her face is covered with a lace veil which reaches to her waist. As the four-woman choir sings *Ave Maria*, the couple bow low to the congregation. They are seconds away from realising their life-long ambition, to walk the Virgin Road, the central aisle of the chapel, and to be married in a Christian wedding ceremony.

Waiting for the couple at the end of the road is the Englishman, Chris, in a flashy golden gown with a silk stole. Chris begins by 'announcing' the wedding and saying the name of the bride and groom very carefully, 'so that I don't get it wrong because that can be a big problem if you do.' Chris has written their names down twice on his script.

The congregation stands and sings hymn No. 320, *What a Friend We Have in Jesus*, in Japanese. The ceremony is roughly sixty per cent in Japanese and forty per cent in English. 'The English is there to add a little bit of exotic flavour to it.'

Chris then reads from Corinthians 13:4, 'Love is gentle, and love is kind…'

'I do that in Japanese first and then in English, and then we do the exchange of vows, "Do you take this man to be your lawful wedded husband", or whatever it is in English. "*Hai, chikaimasu*" [I do].'

RENT A VICAR

Next comes the part the bride has been dreaming about all her life. She turns to the groom who lifts her veil and plants an awkward kiss on her lips. Kissing is a Western concept which was only introduced into Japan after the Second World War. Japanese people dislike seeing or doing it in public, but at a wedding ceremony it is viewed as the height of romantic love. To cover the couple's blushes they have selected a swirling cloud of dry ice from the list of optional extras.

Rings are exchanged and the couple sign the register. At this point, they have chosen another extra: a black gospel soloist singing *You Are So Beautiful* unaccompanied.

Next, Chris says the prayer. For this he prefers to use his own bible. 'It's not too heavy, it's just the right size and it's black. The Jehovah's Witnesses gave it to me when they came to my house a million years ago trying to recruit me.' He places the bible on his lectern and calls the couple forward. 'They put their hands on it and I put my stole on top of their hands and kind of sandwich their hands like that.'

Finally, Chris makes the declaration, the *kekkon sengen*, that the couple are now married. There is applause, and the newlyweds turn to their guests and bow low again. 'And then I do a blessing and that's it, they're out the door.'

As the couple are applauded down the aisle they are covered in another optional extra, the Flower Shower, or petal confetti. It's all over in 17 minutes.

There's just one small issue. Chris didn't marry the couple. Chris isn't a priest. He's not a pastor or a minister or a monk. He has no religious authority whatsoever. He's a 'rent-a-vicar'.

The Japanese wedding industry is a multi-billion yen business, vying for the custom of approximately 700,000 couples a year. Whereas in the West a couple might hire a wedding planner, in Japan the whole day is organised by one-stop bridal companies who own their own mock chapels inside purpose-built wedding 'guesthouses', oversee the catering, rent the bride her gowns, book the MC and the choir, arrange the optional extras, and hire foreigners like Chris.

The most desired wedding is the Disney Royal Dream ceremony offered by Tokyo Disneyland. It takes place in Cinderella Castle where 'your childhood dream of a princess wedding comes true as you spend the day in the magical, dream-like ambience of this wedding program.' The couple get a lot for 7,500,000 yen (approximately £43,000), including a banquet for up to fifty guests, wedding apparel (two sets, each chosen from a range of Disney Princess costumes such as Cinderella, Snow White or Belle), location photographs (three poses), flower arrangements, flower shower, glass place cards, an MC (dressed as a page from Cinderella), and background music. And as a Program Privilege, 'Mickey Mouse, Minnie Mouse, Donald Duck and Daisy Duck will appear dressed up in formal attire at the wedding reception to wish the bride and groom all the best.'

There is no end to the wedding options a couple can choose. But they all have one thing in common. None of them has any legal validity; they are simply parties. To be married in Japan, a couple simply has to sign and submit a piece of paper, a *kekkon todoke*, or marriage registration, at their local ward or city office. By the time the couple take their first steps down the Virgin Road, they are already legally married.

Japan is not a Christian country. Only one per cent of Japan's 127 million population claim to be Christian, yet three-quarters of marrying couples (who decide to have a service) choose a Christian wedding ceremony. Around twelve per cent opt for a Shinto ceremony which, although presided over by a real priest, has no legal authority either. And Shinto ceremonies are not popular with brides because they are only allowed one change of clothing, the traditional white kimono with a white hood to hide their 'horns', a symbol of the inherent evil nature of women. It's no wonder they hold out for the kiss.

Chris has no problem with his job. 'Since there is no legal or religious dimension to the ceremony itself I have no qualms about doing it on any level at all.' Chris arrived in Japan as a backpacker 25 years ago. He teaches English at two high schools, and is the lead singer/guitarist in a rock band called Edward's Operation. For many years he also did talent work; he appeared on commercials and television shows as a foreign face. He got into the wedding business 14 years ago, and is currently employed directly by the Music Grace wedding company, which has its own chapel and banqueting hall in south Tokyo. He gets 7,000 yen (£40) per ceremony which he is not happy about. Additionally, when he started out, he had to buy his own black gown, a cheap import from Korea which cost 15,000 yen (£87). 'It actually cost 10,000 yen (£58) but my boss took 5,000 yen (£29) off the top.'

A few years ago, a reporter from the *Taipei Times* interviewed Chris and then wrote that he and his ilk were frauds. *The Japan Times* called them 'phoney as hell'. The BBC quoted a genuine Japanese Christian priest as saying, 'It is a real problem for us. They are not genuine and they give us a bad name. It is important for the bride and groom to have a proper wedding and they're not getting it from these fake priests.' In fact, it is their Japanese employers who use the term *bokushi* (priest). Chris and his colleagues prefer the English term, 'celebrant'.

Recently Chris's wedding company arranged some kind of tie-up with the local Hase Baptist Church. He believes that the company received a certificate with his name on it and, 'if anyone presses us, we are supposed to answer, "We are attached to this church and therefore we have the right to conduct wedding ceremonies".' In Japan, the whole 'celebrant' issue is as misty as the optional dry ice. But if the ceremony itself is not a legal one and the couple know it, to what extent are Chris and his cohorts deceiving them? If a Japanese couple insist on being married by a genuine priest, can their marriage really be ordained by a Christian God if they themselves are not Christian? Indeed, if the couple aren't Christians, what right have they to demand a genuine priest?

'There is a general move to try and give some authenticity to the celebrants,' says Chris, 'but, in my opinion, it's pretty meaningless because the ceremonies themselves don't have any real meaning. There's no point in trying to pretend that we have some kind of authority or permission to do this.'

Couples are free to choose a Japanese celebrant, especially if they are concerned about the English language sections of the ceremony, but they rarely do. Tall and thin, Chris looks the part of a kindly village curate. 'The point about me of course is that I'm white and so that adds an air of authenticity since obviously the image of it is "the West".'

The White Male is a commodified symbol in Asia, utilised as an image of success and upward mobility in advertising, and to lend authority to corporate and academic settings. White males are seen by many Asian women as more desirable marriage partners than their own countrymen, while Asian businesses note the power of the white man to boost business. In China, for example, there is a fashion for hiring white men as fake partners at business meetings to bring an air of authenticity and make the company appear more international. Called 'white guy window dressing', in the Japanese wedding industry it's what the clients want and the bridal companies must provide. As one prospective groom noted to the BBC, 'It would seem very unreal and fake if there was a Japanese person conducting the ceremony. Very shady actually.'

After the worldwide broadcast of the marriage of Prince Charles to Lady Diana Spencer in 1981, bridal companies were swift to borrow the exotic and sophisticated Christian traditions of the white wedding without much thought as to the religious foundations from which they had grown. Says Chris, 'It's the archetypal form over content thing since it has no meaning whatsoever apart from it looks nice and she wants to wear a white dress.' The walk down the aisle (the Virgin Road), the princess dresses, the prayers, the kiss, the signing of the register and even Chris are there because of the importance to the Japanese of ritual, and of the value placed on the performance of cultural events in a society which is not religious in the Western sense of the word.

'The Japanese like their ceremonies and their meetings and their formal occasions. Just the mere fact of everybody assembling together and going through some form of ritual, the Japanese are particularly keen on that,' says Chris. 'Look at their culture in general, they've got so many events and festivals. And I'm sure this just slots right in there.'

Moreover, Japan's non-legal ceremonies can say more than a legal bond. Indeed, lacking any legal validity, the non-legal ceremony can circumnavigate the law and leap legal loopholes where it lags behind modern mores. In 2012, Disney hosted its first same-sex wedding when a lesbian couple were able to declare their non-legal union to the world with Mickey, Minnie and a

RENT A VICAR

Venetian gondola ride. Those who criticise the 'fake priests' and the mock Christian wedding ceremony are missing the point. It's not about religion, it's not about legality, it's about the public expression of a milestone in life. Chris agrees. 'I'm just providing a service. It doesn't have any religious significance, the ceremonies are not recognised by any churches as having any religious validity, the law doesn't recognise them as having any legal validity so if I can give them a memorable day, something they can look back on with fond memories and some nice photographs, then I feel that my job is done.'

In 2012, the first robot wedding ceremony was held in Japan. The couple walked up the aisle to the tune of *Ave Maria* and were 'married' by an I-Fairy robot wearing a garland of white flowers on its head. As it pronounced the couple man and wife, its eyes flashed green and blue. Chris could soon find himself looking for other part-time work.

Dr Susan K Burton spent 14 years in Japan, lecturing as an associate professor in Japanese universities. She has co-authored two academic books, and is a contributor to *Times Higher* magazine. Her current creative non-fiction project is a collection of essays on the unusual lives and bizarre livelihoods of foreigners in Japan.

LISA CLIMIE

Four Seasons

SPRING – *Child*

AFTER THE SNOW HAD TURNED TO SLUSH, GREEN SHOOTS SLOWLY BEGAN TO APPEAR, FIGHTING THROUGH FROST-CRUSTED EARTH. Snowdrops sprouted in green and white clumps, then yellow and purple crocuses pushed their noses into the sun, while finally groups of daffodils shot up and waved their yellow trumpet heads in the breeze. The thaw revealed the lane which led to my family's new home, invisible for our first eight weeks there after blizzards had cut us off, snow drifting into huge white waves across the lawns, fields and the lane itself. My conscious memories began right then as spring broke, almost as if I had previously existed in a dark room and someone had just flicked on the light.

Soon I began to walk the lane's great length, which felt like many miles, aided by my mother. My little legs, usually stuffed into wellington boots, worked so hard to make their way over its big boulders and to clamber out of its many crevices. The holes in places were so large I thought that if I were to curl up in one I would be hidden from everybody.

Close to our end of the lane was a five-bar gate, the latch of which, climbing up, I would unhook, and then hold on tight as the gate swung back. I would jump off into the ditch before the inevitable jolt as it came to rest, repeating this several times until I tired of pushing it back to the start position. Once through I would hopscotch my way across the holes, kicking loose stones about and jumping on and off the grass ridge that ran down the middle of the lane like a big green vein, often stopping to pick at the hedgerow for flowers, feathers, insects or anything I could spot entwined in its ivy claws.

There was a darker side to the lane though, a side that scared me to my core. For halfway along it, by the turning to Rosiers' Farm, the reds, yellows and pinks of the pretty-but-lethal deadly nightshade lay hidden in the hedgerow. They twinkled in the undergrowth like coloured lanterns; my little fingers reached in, so tempted by them.

'No Lou, you can't eat those, they are poisonous. Witches use them in their nasty potions,' my sister Sarah would warn, pulling my hand away. To my young mind, the rules of country living were often confusing. Life and death co-existed there side by side. Like the birth of lambs in spring and then, months later, the trucks taking them off to slaughter. Attachment was not encouraged and potential dangers needed to be learned well and learned quickly.

SUMMER – *Lover*

Outside my window a Tyrannosaurus Rex sprints across the sky with an arrow in his back. Then he's a horse galloping, breath visibly pouring like vapour from his nostrils. Next he's a cat crouching, ears erect listening for prey, then he's a crocodile skeleton then... gone. All this takes place in the space of a few moments as I gaze out looking for answers.

In the round bedroom, full of fever, I'd drifted in and out of consciousness as the evening summer sun bled across the horizon, staining the sky pink then orange then red.

Day to night, night to day, but which is which? Every time I woke there you were, dressed in black, thick hair dark and unruly, coffee in one hand, joint in the other. The joint went out repeatedly as the conversation, the flame and your face floated around me. Was I stoned or just delirious?

You'd invited me a few weeks before to come to your show.

Then that Black Widow Spider – your 'Last Rider', still holding on – had appeared and caused a scene. You had looked at me and shrugged – 'Sorry,' while she was strutting up and down, mouth wide and thoughtless, arms flailing around. I'd left.

I had thought then I should not get involved, would never get involved. I looked on at the triangle you lived in, and could never imagine myself in such a place.

You talked of the Island, of the summer days and of the big flood, of your dreams, of India and of Paradise. You told me of the Sagas and spoke the beginning of *Authun and the Bear* in Old Icelandic. You were a magician pulling Shakespeare, Milton and Blake out of your hat and mixing them up with amphetamine Burroughs, rat-a-tat-tat, rat-a-tat-tat.

Or reciting in long drooling Dylan tones:

'How does it feee-yel? How does it feee-yel?' You ask,
about my brand new leopard-skin pillbox hat.
Or pleading with me to – 'Craa-wel' out my window,
'It won't ruin yoouu,' you say.
'Use your arms and leeegs,' you say.
Your words leave me spellbound.

But can I really come back to you anytime I want to?

Night to day, day to night – it was all the same to you, who didn't sleep. Sometime in that dream which came and went through those few days, I stepped up on the bank and looked across the water with you, floated above it on the clouds with you, looked back and saw that everything else was very small and unfamiliar. I mistook my damaged teenage heart for a strong vessel, not the patched up leaking life raft it was.

You kept vigil by my bed and with tender song embraced me with your words, played me with your touch, and caressed me with your lips. All resistance drained away, all caution already fled, all fear abandoned: there would be no turning back if I said yes.

You asked as though a formal proposal, 'Will you be my girlfriend?'

A final disarming moment, before I heard that little word, that small, bright, quick little word, leap from my lips – 'Yes.'

FOUR SEASONS

AUTUMN – *Son*

The high days and holidays of my teens and twenties passed by in a haze, more highs than holidays. Then, like a fermenting apple I fell with a thud and lay helpless and bruised on the sun-charred ground.

Bob told us – the times they are a-changing – and I realised I would have to change too if I were to reach maturity.

I scrambled and crawled through the undergrowth searching for a path; brambles tore at my skin, tugged at my hair and snaking tree roots lassoed my feet again and again along the way. I found a freshwater stream, and lay down and watched as it turned from a muddy trickle to a flowing rush of clarifying life.

Stevie called out to me – not waving but drowning – so was I too far out?

I felt the water rise; I let it flow over me, slowly it ground down and polished my sharp edges. I was able to stand once more on solid earth, raising my sight from ground to sky, for the first time looking life straight in the eye.

William told me – the road of excess leads to the palace of wisdom. He was right of course, but not in the way I had imagined.

*

Following the pruning, ploughing and planting, the watering, feeding and the sun warming I had come to full bloom. My rounded belly held the future, all hope and wonder. I would never again experience being just me, from now on there would always be you too. You were the harvest, the bounty, the prize.

A deep and vibrant palette painted our canvas with ancient hues; gold ochre, burnt umber and cadmium red flashed and turned. Warm air swam about us and all living things hummed, whispered and sang:

> *Speed bonnie boat like a bird on the wing,*
> *Onward the sailors cry,*
> *Carry the lad that is born to be King,*

LISA CLIMIE

Over the seas to Skye.

Autumn was the first full season we shared. It was full of plenty. At the equinox the swelling harvest moon reached fullness.

For three long nights it cast a warm orange glow upon us as we danced and crops were gathered to sustain us. I sang to you:

Dance t' thy daddy, my little laddie
Dance t' thy daddy, ti' thy mammy sing
When thou art an old man, father to a son
Sing to him the old songs, sing of all you've done.

WINTER – *Mother*

My final season is yet to come. I hope it will not come too soon as there is so much more I want to see, hear and feel. So much I need to learn, to explore and to tell.

Your winter came early and was long and dark. I was too young when I walked through it with you. I did not then have the strength I now have, to face the harshness of that cold and dying season. To witness you, who had given me life, lose your vibrant colour, your budding brilliance, your oozing sap.

Remembering now, visiting you as the days shortened and darkened.

You're sleeping, that's a relief. I know I'm late. I had to stop on the way.

You see, the truth is, I just can't face you. Can't face what you have become.

The drink takes the edge off. But then it makes it worse too. I know when you smell it on my breath, you know why. You know I find it hard to look at you.

Those bent crooked hands, trying to drink from a baby's beaker; your pillow-matted hair, your weak drugged voice, your steroid-swollen face, your bed, surrounded by bags and rubbish like a tramp in the subway. The smell of stale milk in the bottom of the plastic bag you carry on your Zimmer frame. Those maggots, oh God those maggots

FOUR SEASONS

I found in the bag that day. The vile smell and the picture of that squirming mass will never leave me.

Twenty-six springs, twenty-six summers, twenty-six autumns and twenty-six winters have passed since you left. Through them all I have followed your ages as I pass through each. I have experienced motherhood myself and understand you anew. Now I know to be perfect is not to be human, that it is through each seasonal cycle that we grow and we cannot remain in just one; spring will always turn to summer and autumn leaves must always turn and fall.

If I close my eyes I can go back. I remember your wide smile, your full husky Tabasco laugh, the way you held your cigarette aloft in prideful and elegant defiance. Your rich flaming auburn hair, cut into your nape, when no one else did that. Your sense of drama and fashion bravery, that time you went to a dinner party dressed in a gold sari, or your favourite shocking pink scarf around your neck. Your chunky Maltese Cross hanging down, nestling between your breasts.

And your sweet-perfumed handkerchief a balm as you wiped your lipstick from my small, resistant face.

Lisa Climie, as a memoirist, depicts a life spent in the world of entertainment. She touches on her magical, sometimes tragic and often unorthodox experiences. As a biographer, Lisa was commissioned by the T E Lawrence Society Journal to write *Shadow Man*, an 8,000-word article about her great uncle's close friendship with Lawrence.

HANNAH CONEYS

The Thirteenth Stage

The Tour de France, 1967: Tom Simpson chases immortality on Mont Ventoux

ON A YACHT IN MARSEILLES MARINA, WITH A BRICK-SIZED CHUNK OF ICE STABBED ON A FORK BETWEEN THEM, Tom Simpson and Barry Hoban pantomimed the extraordinary heat of that summer. They licked the ice like a gigantic lolly, Barry with some embarrassment and Tom, whose idea it most likely was, gurning with his tongue sticking out grotesquely. Barry then pretended to throw Tom into the water.

Jean Bobet was among the crowd of journalists. Once a Tour winner himself, he was now a correspondent for *L'Equipe*. Two years previously Bobet had photographed Tom after he had become the first Briton to win a stage, and had posed him in his clean new yellow jersey, with a bowler hat and umbrella, prancing on the stairs: an Englishman in Paris.

Tom was halfway through his fourth Tour de France. At 4,780 kilometres it was the longest that there had ever been, and five of his ten British teammates had already dropped out. Perhaps he looked a little leaner than usual in the press photographs, but then he lived on a strict diet shored up by carrot juice and fresh vegetables, which, mercifully, were cheaper in the markets of Ghent than in his native Harworth. His deep-set eyes looked dark, his sharp nose and cheekbones prominent against his thin face. But he was still smiling, even with a mouth full of ice.

THE THIRTEENTH STAGE

He had started this Tour with a strict plan. He and his team would focus their attention on three major mountain stages, with the intention of either standing on the podium on the Champs Elysees, or collecting a few yellow jerseys along the way. On the first of these stages, climbing the Col du Galibier, he had suffered from diarrhoea and dropped from sixth to sixteenth place. Before the Tour began, the assembled journalists had predicted that he would finish eleventh. He looked forward to proving them wrong.

Tomorrow they would pass over Mont Ventoux, where Ferdi Kübler's career had come to an abrupt end in 1955. Tom knew the story well; as a child his bedroom had been decorated with pictures of the one-time Tour winner. The Swiss had begun the stage full of hubris. 'The Ventoux is not like any other col,' his teammate warned him. 'Ferdi's not like the other riders,' he replied. Leading the race alone Ferdi found himself dehydrated, and stopped to find a beer. By the time he reached the summit he was delirious and began to cycle back the way he had come. A spectator tried to set him on the correct course but he pushed them away, shouting, 'Get out of the way, leave me, Ferdi's going crazy, Ferdi's going to explode!' That evening he announced his retirement from the sport with the words, 'Ferdi has killed himself on the Ventoux.'

Tomorrow Tom would have the chance to conquer the mountain that had conquered Ferdi Kübler. It was his second. Two years previously he had passed over the Ventoux in the rear of the peloton, with an infected wound and the beginnings of bronchitis. Now he began to bear a superficial hatred of every person who stood between him and victory. 'I can get the buggers back,' he told Harry, his mechanic, as they prepared his bike that evening. 'When they sit on my wheel I'll blow their brains out. I'll get the bastards.'

Harry cared diligently for Tom. He would work through the night, modifying the bike – once he fashioned him a more comfortable saddle from the leather of Mrs Helen Simpson's crocodile handbag – and accompanied him on every stage, riding behind him in the team car.

After the Col du Galibier, Tom's bike had been sent back to

Harry for cleaning and he could see from its state that the rider was seriously unwell. At the marina Barry gently encouraged him to take the next day slowly, but his suggestion was met with anger. His boss, Gaston Plaud, told him the same in stronger terms: 'You must stop racing this Tour de France for the sake of your health. This is no good.' Again Tom refused to listen. The Ventoux was the mountain on which a cyclist became great, and physical suffering was part of the exchange. 'I think it's riding the Tour that makes a cyclist immortal,' he had said in a recent interview. He had stages like this one in mind.

The riders hung on the start line. Tom inspected his bike, checked his brakes. He wore the uniform of his team: a thin woollen jersey, white, with his number pinned on its back; black woollen shorts; a cloth cap; leather loafers. The last time he had attacked the Ventoux his shorts had become so saturated with sweat that they had fallen down.

Harry had re-taped his handlebars to create the illusion of a fresh bike. The machine smelled of grease. He got on and Harry strapped Tom's feet to the pedals.

Jean Bobet caught Tom's eye from behind the barrier. Tom attempted to return his smile, but to Bobet it looked more like a grimace. Then Tom stuck his tongue out, and he saw five white pills on it. The front of the field began to filter out, to the cheers of the crowd, and the figure bearing the number 49 was obscured.

Though no one cared to break the code of silence, everyone knew about Tom's use of *la moutarde*, or his 'Mickey Finns,' as he called them: he would arrive at the team's hotel with two suitcases, one for his clothes and the other for the drugs and their accoutrements. Those doctors who were in on the scheme recommended a maximum intake of eight milligrams of Tonedron per dose, but the body grew resistant to it over time, and Tom was adventurous. He had once given some to a dog at a friend's party. It had survived, and it was small.

Cicadas called out from the dry fields. He hated that sound; he hated the heat. Having learned to ride in Yorkshire, cold and wet was his preference. The sun made his bike frame hot to the touch.

THE THIRTEENTH STAGE

Tom, like every competitor, carried only two small bottles of water with him. Popular wisdom held that the energy spent processing water could be better used in the legs. *La chasse à la canette* became a tradition of the race, when parched team leaders would dispatch their *domestiques* to beg for a drink from homes or cafés.

Colin Lewis found a restaurant by the roadside. By the time he caught up with Tom in the breakaway both were parched. Tom grabbed the bottle of Coke and drank half straight off. He passed the rest back to Colin.

'What else have you got?' he asked.

Colin pulled the second bottle from his jersey pocket. It was brandy, and half full.

'My guts aren't feeling too good, give us a swig,' said Tom and drank half of it, then cycled hard.

An hour later Tom was watching the breakaway leave him behind. He had stuck with them to the foothills of the mountain, through heat that had made the liquid food curdle in his bottle. As the road steepened in the intermittent shade of the forest he noticed that he was slowing down. Bright light flickered through the pines, making him feel sick. His stomach hurt.

In the shade of the forest he saw a hut. He pulled over, flung his bike onto the verge and went in.

From the roof of the team car where he was setting up his camera, Harry recognised Tom's bike. He called for the driver to stop as Tom emerged from the trees, screwing the lid back on his bottle. Harry felt sure that it did not contain water.

'Hey, Tom, that's naughty, you shouldn't be doing that,' he called out.

Tom winked, got back on his bike and cycled on, swigging at the cognac in his bottle.

The three tubes of pills rattled together inside his jersey. Two were empty now. His mouth was dry, and it was hard to focus his eyes. He rode hunched forward, his saddle higher than his handlebars; his head bobbed forward with each revolution of the pedals.

Spectators in sun hats lined the road. One man strode out in front of him and threw a cupful of water into his face, a violent act of kindness. Tom's body had no more sweat in it.

Team cars and lone cyclists passed him. The peloton could not be far behind. He leaned forwards for another push and gripped his curved handlebars. The forest began to fade away and the summit, seeming snowy but shimmering with heat, stared him down. As he drew near to the tree line a hot wind threw grit into his open mouth.

The mountain hummed with heat. In his white jersey Tom faded into the landscape as he rode out of the shade. The rise in temperature was instant and he breathed dry dust as he tried to fill his lungs. At 1,900 metres above sea level, the air yielded little oxygen. Ahead were the insect-like forms of the breakaway group.

The French cyclist Lucien Aimar gained on Tom, and saw that his eyes were glazed. He drew level and offered Tom some water, but he did not acknowledge him and instead tried to cycle away. Aimar encouraged him to hang back and rest in his slipstream for a while, but Tom appeared not to have heard him.

'Tom, stop fooling about,' he said. Tom cycled on.

Two kilometres from the summit he began to serpentine across the road, first veering left until inches from the sheer cliff, then to the bank on the other side. His head bobbed from side to side as if encouraging each leg in turn.

From the team car Harry saw that Tom was about to fall. They pulled over and he ran to him, in time to catch the bike. He tried to lay Tom down.

'No, no, no, up, up,' rambled Tom. Unsure of what to do, Harry began to steer Tom along the road.

'Me straps, Harry,' said Tom, and Harry tied his feet back onto the pedals. Tom slowly pedalled away, and Harry heard his words echo back to him from the rocks: 'On, on, on, on, on.'

Two topless men on the roadside saw Tom lean forward on his handlebars and curve to the right. His legs were no longer turning the pedals but his dry, yellow hands gripped the bike tightly. As the bike began to topple they caught it and guided it to the side of the road. Harry ran to them and untied the straps on the feet. He tried to carry Tom on his back, but he was limp and heavy. They laid him down, legs in the road and head on a pillow of stones. His hands had to be prised from the handlebars. Harry tried to give Tom chest compressions, but the air that was drawn into his lungs simply left again with a sickening wheeze.

The Tour physician and a nurse drew up in their car. The nurse began to blow air into Tom's mouth. Her hand on his face pushed the eyelids back slightly.

A crowd gathered on the slope above them. They stood at a respectful distance, for the most part.

The doctor unzipped Tom's jersey and the three tubes of pills fell out. He continued to treat the body until a helicopter came to take it away.

Bobet was struck by the perfection of the silence as the typewriters stopped clicking in the press room. Some of the journalists went down to the morgue to view the body and the silence followed them there. Tom's body lay on a trolley, half-covered by a sheet. His eyes were still open. One photographer took pictures of the body. 'I'm sorry,' he said after every exposure.

Hannah Coneys is writing a group biography of three cyclists whose lives changed on Mont Ventoux. A vicarage child who lived briefly in an international Christian community, Hannah is also investigating the Burmese Church. She lives in Cambridge with her husband – yet another vicar. She has also published fictional works.

CATHERINE CONROY

A House

*Following the death of her mother, a young woman
seeks out a new home*

I BOUGHT THE HOUSE EIGHT YEARS AGO WHEN I THOUGHT I WAS GOING MAD. My mother had died, and I was fine initially. I was grand for about a year, to be honest. I remember my boss asking me how I was coping and I said, 'I feel sort of invincible. The worst thing has happened to me and I can still get up out of bed.' But then I began to feel sick on the bus to work in the mornings and, thinking I was going to vomit into the laps of old ladies with tartan trolleys, I'd stare at my shoes and breathe deeply. A lot of the advice on the internet was about breathing. When that didn't work, I'd have to get off at any old stop. I started walking everywhere, but often, like an old film, it felt like I was standing still while the background was moving. Breathe, I'd say to myself. In a restaurant with friends, I'd be very quiet and when I finally thought to speak, the words sounded like they'd been flung in the air and had fallen with a clatter on the table. I'd look at the faces around me for reaction, then turn to my closest friend and whisper, 'Did that sound OK? Did that sound strange?'

I took sudden exits off motorways. I took Xanax before I went to the pub. I spent my weekends in bookshops, for the silence of them, but also to look for assurance in the pages that this had happened to others. I watched the world for a message from my mother. I felt it was the least she could do. But there were no watercolour dreams, no white feather drifting slowly down, no strange bird perched at an opportune moment. I went to sleep at night clutching her old holy medal, and woke up with the deep sweaty imprint of it on my palm.

I went to a doctor and told her I was on the way to the mental hospital. She took out her prescription pad and said, 'Truly mad people don't know they're going mad. This is just grief, and long overdue.' She sent me to a therapist. I took anti-depressants.

Then I got the idea into my head that the real problem was a lack of refuge. I'd grown up in a house that was always warm and softly lit. There were the usual strains and shouting, but it was a safe place. We were an intact family with a shaggy dog. But after Mam's long painful illness, with the morphine and the commode, and then the long rowdy wake, there was a terrible silence in the rooms and I stopped going back to visit. And now I felt like I had nowhere to go. The flats I rented around Dublin had no permanence to them. I decided I would buy a house. The banks were flinging money at us at the time. I'd build myself a fort.

It was a Saturday in the summer when I first went to view it. I walked the length of the horseshoe-shaped road, to the far end where the house stood. The nature of the road changed as I walked, starting out with well-minded houses with gardens full of pink roses and chrysanthemums, quaint little gates and railings at the steps. Towards the middle of the hoop, there were 'Beware of the Dog' signs, bad paint jobs, the occasional daub of graffiti on a garage door. Everything looked a bit battered and grey. But as I came to the last leg of the road, the houses spruced themselves up again and as I reached No. 286, the day brightened and the sky was blue and, beyond the football pitch at the bottom of the road, you could see the purple mountains framed by the white goalposts. Many a house and owner must be brought together by the good fortune of a sunny day. It was a two-storey house at the end of a terrace, newly-built on a corner plot. There were mature plants in the small front garden, a broken 'For Sale' sign, a tall palm tree in the corner. The driveway was paved with red brick and covered in the crunch of fallen fronds.

I moved in before I had any furniture and I spent the first night on my own in a sleeping bag in the corner of the sitting room, like a squatter. Without curtains or carpets, every noise echoed. I walked around with a small camera and showed myself the empty rooms. The blinds were pulled down and there were no lampshades, only bare bulbs giving out dim light. I sat on the wooden floor that still had some spring and still hadn't settled, and I filmed myself. 'This is your new home,' I said into the camera, the way a mother might talk to a newborn.

Things were good for a while. A house is a very distracting thing and you can build and build upon it. When I was a kid, Mam was always decorating. By the time she had done every room in our home, the first room would be outdated, and it would need paint now instead of wallpaper, wooden floors instead of carpets; endless rearranging. I took some of Mam's old stuff now, things I thought Dad might not appreciate: an old Roberts radio, a small antique chair she'd upholstered, china cups she'd found in bric-a-brac shops. I put them with my new things. I bought a beautiful big bed, a dark wood dressing table with an age-speckled mirror, an old trunk with shipping stickers. In my new bedroom, the curtains and blinds were white and kept out little light, so the mornings were undeniable. It was like sleeping in a tent. On Sunday afternoons, I would walk around garden centres in a state of grace, fondling the pansies.

All the local kids hung around on my corner and sat on my wall. They were aged around ten or twelve – it's hard to know. Night after night, their football would wallop against the side of the house and the side of my car. I would wrap my dressing gown tight around me and go out and say, 'Lads, come on, go easy will you.' It would stop briefly. Then they would light little fires in the bushes out the front that wouldn't really take, but would smoulder enough to carry a smell into the house and make me rush out. It was a rare night when there was nothing happening, and even in the silence I'd get up and check anyway in case there was some stealth operation at play. There was a mix of girls and boys initially. The girls were easily bought off. I had a bag of old make-up I was throwing out that I gave to them and they went away. But the boys were less partial to bribery. I tried sweets, I tried chattiness, I tried to be a bit cool. I once even managed to get them to paint over their own graffiti on my garden gate. I supervised them, handing out paintbrushes, and more boys came and asked could they join in too. One wee fella got to his painstaking work with a tiny eyeshadow brush I found for him at the back of a drawer. There I was in the middle of them, the Great White Hope.

But then the windows. They smashed the little one on the landing first, and that one would go again and again. Then I came home from a week away and a huge terracotta pot from the garden had been hurled through the large front window so that the living room was full of broken glass and soil and cold air. I sat down on the sofa for a moment and looked at the mess, stunned by the insistence of the outside world. The neighbours said they saw nothing. When I called the guards to talk about it, they'd tell me about the families around there in varying states of despair; kids who had been to court, been assigned liaison officers at nine years old. What could I say? I was sorry, but I only wanted a bit of peace. The guards would sometimes patrol the road, but I heard them joke with the boys, reprimand them like indulgent parents.

One boy called Shotgun kept tagging the gable end of my house, huge black lettering, nothing particularly artistic. Each night on my way home from work, my bus passed a grotto near the entrance to the estate. The blue and white of Virgin Mary was washed off and she stood there grey, hands clasped, eyes heavenward. 'Give me a fuckin' break tonight Mary, will ya?' I'd think to myself. Then I'd come round the corner and see Shotgun's big mad scrawl. I kept a tub of paint under the kitchen sink, and late at night when all the kids had been swept away from the corners, I'd go out in my old tracksuit bottoms and, by the orange glow of the street light, I'd paint the wall white again.

The night I decided to leave, I was lying on the sofa in my pyjamas and there was a loud banging on the window. I froze and put the telly on mute. I ran up the stairs to the landing to look out the window there where no one would see me, and in the dark I could make out a boy walking along the high wall at the side of the house. With a small jump, he got on to the flat roof of the kitchen and started stomping on it. I went back downstairs and stood in my nice white kitchen looking at the ceiling. There was another set of feet, and then a storm of them. I called the guards but I knew that by the time they'd arrive, the boys would have legged it through the back gardens in the estate, ducking under the football jerseys and the sheets on the clothes lines. Suddenly, there was silence and then the doorbell rang. I went to the door and opened it. Shotgun was standing there, only up to my shoulder in height. He was acting the mick for some other fellas who were crouched behind the wall laughing. He said, 'I'm here for the party' and he made to come in and tried to dart around me into the warm house. I got him by the shoulders and gave him an almighty shove and he tripped back and fell down off the step. His hands went back to the ground either side of him to take the fall. His wrists bent back with the weight. And the two of us stayed like that. Me, standing in the frame of the front door, the house lit behind me, the beige carpet dirty now on the stairs, waiting for him to move, shocked at myself. Him, lying there in the driveway. He got up slowly and grabbed at his wrist, curling his fingers around it, wriggling it in his other hand. He looked at me with the fury that comes to cover up pain.

You fucking whale, he said, you crazy bitch. Fuck off back to where you came from.

And then lots of little boys stood up from behind the white garden wall to look at us, the shadows of them with their hoods up round their heads, the strings pulled tight so that only their eyes and noses could be seen. Shotgun pulled up his own hood with his good hand and disappeared into the middle of them, still shouting. I went in and waited for a while, sitting on the arm of the sofa, for a visit from a furious father, or a scrappy mother, or the guards. But no one came.

Catherine Conroy is a solicitor from Dublin. Her work has been published in *The Irish Times* and *The Dublin Review*. She is currently working on *The Dead Mothers Club*, an exploration of grief and friendship, and *Redress*, based on her professional experience fighting for compensation for church abuse victims.

JOHN DENNEHY

Illegal

Love, revolution and deportation

TWO POLICEMEN GRABBED ME BY THE SHOULDERS and pulled me away from the immigration counter at Quito International Airport.

'*¿Qué hice?*' I asked, my voice shaking.

I tried to see their faces but the police turned from me. They each jabbed an arm in the space between my arm and torso, curled their elbow under my armpit and locked their hand on my shoulder. Now facing the opposite direction from me, they marched forward, pushing my upper body with them and forcing my feet to backpedal. A third officer walked in front, leading us against the flow of passengers moving toward passport control.

'*¿Qué hice yo?*' I asked louder, almost shouting.

Silence.

'*¿Qué hice?!*'

People were staring at us but the police just walked forward, dragging me with them. I turned my head and saw a half dozen more officers. They were standing under the staircase in the corner of the massive room, keeping an eye on us as we approached.

When we reached the larger group the two police holding me relaxed their grip. The one on my right took a step back to face me. He was young, about my age, and his crisp, olive green hat was too small for his head. He looked down to avoid my eyes and told me, '*Usted estará en nuestra custodia hasta que se vuelan de regreso a Estados Unidos. Yo no te puedo decir nada más*' – You will be in our custody until you are flown back to the United States. I can't tell you anything else. He paused before adding, 'I'm sorry.'

I saw an opening. I knew the police didn't want a scene.

'*Necesito ver mi novia*' – I need to see my girlfriend. The words rushed out. 'She's waiting for me and won't know what happened.'

I had seen her on my way in, standing behind the pane of glass that separated a small food court from the long hallway toward immigration control. She was holding a sunflower and waving, smiling, waiting. I kept playing that scene back in my head. Kept wondering where she was now, what she was thinking. She would have seen everyone from my flight pass through. Maybe she was already piecing things together. She still had a copy of my passport and instructions for whom to call if I was arrested – souvenirs from our trouble at the Colombian border a month before when the overweight officer in Ecuador threatened me with five years in jail if I tried to sneak in.

My mind flashed between her two faces: waving at me from behind the glass, smiling and excited; sitting at arrivals, biting her lip like she did before she cried.

Six months before, when the 'Citizen's Revolution' began and all the highways were blockaded, she came for me. I had spent the day at a seized bridge downtown, talking with the rebels and trying to understand why they were willing to risk so much to prevent a free-trade agreement with the United States. All the schools and businesses were closed either out of solidarity or fear and Lucía spent the day hitchhiking through the rebels' barricades so we could be together during the chaos. I already knew parts of her complicated past by then; a month before that she had started to reveal to me the various layers of her broken marriage. When we collapsed onto my bed that night, still coughing from the tear gas lingering over the city, I decided that if we could be together that day, then we would be on every day to come.

'I need to see my girlfriend,' I said to no one in particular, scanning the faces of the police. The passengers waiting in line had stared when the uniformed men pushed me across the room but their attention passed quickly. I could see people thumbing through passports, inching forward, oblivious.

'I need to see my girlfriend,' I said again, louder, loud enough for others to hear. I was on the verge of screaming, and could feel myself beginning to tremble. 'I live here. I work here. And I need to see my girlfriend!'

Passengers walking past slowed down and looked on curiously. No police were holding me but they formed a perimeter around my body. When I shouted they all took a step in, tightening the circle. I could smell their cologne and sweat above the sterile monotony of airport disinfectant. Passengers stopped and stared. Some already in line looked back.

'I didn't do anything wrong! Please, I need to see my girlfriend.'

My mind raced back to the argument we'd had the night before my trip, to the insults we threw at each other. It made me that much more desperate to see her, to whisper in her ear that I still loved her, that I would always love her.

A lot of passengers were watching. I lowered my voice and stared at the officer in front of me, the one who led the two police from the counter. His dark brown eyes stared back. He blinked and I could see tiny wrinkles branch out in fine lines as his eyelids shut.

'What's her name?' he asked.

'Lucía. She has black hair, black jeans and is wearing a white T-shirt with hearts – she's holding a sunflower.'

'I'll look for her,' he said, then quickly walked away.

I sat down on the cold tiled floor and the remaining police relaxed. The passengers moved on.

I didn't know how it would work out. I was about to move in with the girl that I loved and was directly involved with a revolution that was not just changing my adoptive nation, but was changing me. For the first time in my life I knew exactly where I wanted to be. I had found my home in the shadow of an Andean volcano in Ecuador – but it was all in peril. I thought about how I would find another professor to cover my classes at the university, and how I would get rent money to my landlord, but my thoughts always drifted back to Lucía.

I jumped to my feet when I saw her. My impulse was to run toward her, but the uniforms around me closed the circle again. I stood still and watched her walk toward me. Her eyes were red and she wiped away the tears when she got near.

ILLEGAL

The police opened the circle, allowing her to pass, then closed it again, trapping us both inside. She threw her arms around me and created a bubble. Nothing else was real, nothing else mattered. For a moment, the world did not exist. We were silent. My hands slid down her body and rested on the small of her back. My fingers pulled on her shirt, bunching it into a ball inside my fist. We had instinctively moved our bodies against each other; our legs intertwined and her breasts pressed against me. Our faces touched and I felt her warm skin against mine, our tears mixing on each other's cheeks. I closed my eyes and inhaled through my nostrils, smelling her sweet perfume, remembering the taste of her neck. We lifted our heads and touched our lips, opening, tasting each other's salt.

When we returned our heads to each other's shoulders we let the water run. It's hard to match my memory with reality because it seems so surreal now. The image of Lucía and the thought of seeing her had kept me focused and held me together. Once she was in my arms I let go. The tears did not streak into droplets; they flowed down my cheek in a steady stream. Our mouths, next to each other's ears, whispered '*te amo*' over and over again. I knew the police would soon separate us. I knew nothing would ever be the same again. I felt helpless and overwhelmed, as if drowning in slow motion.

The first action I took, the first thing that wasn't reflexive, was to whisper in her ear the plan I had hastily worked out minutes before. '*Voy a volar a Colombia y cruzar la frontera clandestinamente. Nada más importa. Te amo*' – I will fly to Colombia and sneak across the border. Nothing else matters. I love you.

Lucía stepped back and pulled a camera from her bag. The movement, the loss of her body against mine, jolted me back into reality. The police were all staring at us, peering into what had seemed such a private and intimate place just seconds before. Lucía handed one of our guards the camera and, for some strange reason, had him take a picture of us and freeze that moment in time.

In the photo we have our arms around each other, our eyes, red from sobbing, are looking right into the lens. That's the moment I broke. Sure, I could will myself to wipe away the tears and look into the camera, but deep down, deeper than I would comprehend for months to come, there was no pretending.

When I moved to Latacunga, a wave began to build. Every morning I walked upstairs and looked past the red-tiled roofs of the colonial center and toward Cotopaxi, the 19,000-foot snow-capped volcano that dominated the landscape. Each afternoon I pedaled my bike to the city's edge to work in a converted prison. Before I had arrived, during the jail's construction, locals had risen up in protest so forcefully that the government had no choice but to meet their demands. The walls were repainted and it became one of the first free universities in the nation, a radical concept that was growing quickly. At night, I laid down with Lucía and fell asleep to her heart beating against mine. I had wiped the water away for the picture but I could still taste the salt from the first splash of that wave breaking.

'We have to move,' the officer with the dark brown eyes said. The same two police grabbed my shoulders and pulled me away.

Thirty days before I met the president; six weeks before Lucía told me her husband had hired a hitman; three months before I walked away from the barricades and decided to fight against the revolution rather than for it; half a year before I gave up – I was deported.

John Dennehy grew up in New York but moved out of the US when President Bush was re-elected. For five years he lived in Latin America, returning to the United States in 2010. He is writing a book titled *Illegal*, about his deportation from Ecuador.

DEBORAH JAY

The Watercolourist

TRAINING, ACUMEN AND AN ILL-STARRED CONSTELLATION WOULD TAKE GIOVANNI BATTISTA LUSIERI IN LATE NOVEMBER 1799, a historic moment in the course of Anglo-French conflict, from celebrity to ignominy and set in motion a struggle which still dogs Britain today. His pivotal and yet tragic role in the extraction of what are now known as the Elgin Marbles, acquired by the British Museum in 1816, remains largely unacknowledged.

According to the diocesan register, Giovanni Battista Callisto Giustino Baldassare was immersed in the baptismal font of the Basilica of St Peter's in Rome a few days after he was born on 14 October 1754. His father, Mattia Lusieri, a silversmith from Pesaro, had come to Rome three years earlier with his wife, son and daughter. Little is known about Giovanni Battista's early years. The imagination has to conjure his world.

At that time, the Eternal City comprised some hundred and sixty thousand souls huddled together in the area defined by the Porta del Popolo, the old Forum Boarium, the Trastevere, the Tiber, the Baths of Diocletian and the slopes of the Hill of the Quirinale within the ancient Aurealian wall. Rome was generally safe, thieving, kidnap and abduction practically unknown. There is nothing to suppose that Giovanni Battista had anything other than an unexceptional eighteenth-century Roman childhood. On that assumption, he spent the mornings receiving some formal if ineffectual education, largely in Latin, from friars of one of the local orders learned in dogma. In all likelihood, he spent much of the rest of his time in his father's workshop. He saw how to fashion all manner of silverwork. Most popular were crosses, chalices, precious reliquaries and ritual objects for use in church, tea services, forks and spoons. Also in demand were salvers, bowls, chains, snuffboxes, whistles, mechanical utensils, swords, bridle buckles and saddle nails, and accessories for sedans and other conveyances. His father might also have made agricultural and surgical implements, and components for ships and weaponry. He would have worked not only in silver, but in many metals – principally copper, brass and gold – and with precious gems of agate, amethyst and rubies. The workshop buzzed with activity, pervaded by the smell of sweat and molten ore, hot from the furnaces. The din of pounding and teasing of metal was unrelenting, concentration punctuated intermittently by short exchanges or expletives when material proved resistant or lack of care caused waste. Such specialised expertise required time, infinite patience and a calm temperament. Having laboured hard to obtain the stamp of approval in the form of an official silver mark from the Papal authorities, Mattia watched everyone closely, anxious to maintain high standards of craftsmanship. Working fast was scorned: Rome waited for excellence, a stranger to deadlines.

The young Giovanni Battista started helping his father with small items requiring repair or alteration. Then, having begun to show some promise as a draughtsman, the novice progressed to preparing designs for customer requests. A steady hand was required for engraving monograms, family crests and inscriptions. Increasingly essential to the silversmith's trade in the second half of the eighteenth century was a printing press. Prints were used routinely for silverwork commissions and for notices, labels and illustrations. In his father's workshop, Giovanni Battista learned precision and a high degree of finish required at various stages of the process of silversmithing. He also understood the commercial side of the trade, the management and flattering of clients, the importance of being on good terms with everyone and of keeping tight control over finances. This preparation was to stand him in good stead, though he would not necessarily recognise when enough was enough.

As Giovanni Battista reached adolescence, his father sent him out to make deliveries on a horse and cart, typically shared with neighbouring trades. These jaunts revealed to him the world between the confines of the alleys around the Castel Sant'Angelo, the countryside and possibly the other towns within a day's journey from Rome, like Frascati or Castelgandolfo, locations of the Pope's summer residences.

Working days, of which there were barely one hundred and fifty in the year after taking account of religious holidays, started around eight in the morning and ended around eight at night, allowing for the obligatory, often lengthy siesta. During the afternoon when the city was asleep, Giovanni Battista wandered out along narrow lanes beyond his parents' modest three-storey house near the Ponte Sant'Angelo. Loitering around churches, fountains and squares, he was fascinated by the artists, mostly foreign, who had set up their easels to record the architectural feast before them. Some could speak a smattering of the Italian language as spoken in Tuscany, having studied the texts of Boccaccio and Dante. Others conversed in Latin with the factotums who helped them carry, load and unload equipment and run errands.

Perhaps the aspiring watercolourist caught the attention of one of the foreign gentlemen artists on the Piazza Navona or at the base of the Spanish Steps and engaged in conversation. Possibly a more consummate artist gave him the benefit of his experience. Whatever the influences, he soon began to demonstrate a clear preference for sketching sculpture over portraiture.

The steady trickle of *milords*, as the Romans called the foreigners, which had started some twenty years before Giovanni Battista was born, began to increase when the fragments of the *Forma Urbis Romae*, the ancient city plan engraved in the 3rd Century CE, was exhibited at the Capitoline Museum in 1741. The Bourbon king, Charles III, had found the Severan Marble Plan when packing up his inheritance in Parma to transfer his capital and court to the Bay of Naples. For the first time, Romans were able to see how Rome had existed at the height of its prosperity in ancient times. It was clear that there might lie undiscovered much more of the remains of the city's former splendour than the naked eye could see.

Idealistic, mostly aristocratic and frequently ill-informed travellers were the pioneers of what became known as the

Grand Tour. This trajectory soon constituted an indispensable rite of passage for the educated of means in Northern Europe, particularly those of a literary or artistic bent. Covering their mouths and noses with Brussels lace handkerchiefs, they baulked at the malodour – *l'aria cattiva*. Giovanni Battista and his compatriots were rarely ill and thought the pestilential air, to which the tourists were much more vulnerable, positively beneficial to well-being. Newly arrived visitors were aghast at the largely unpaved roads, thick with dust in heat and mud in rain, the gutters suppurating with refuse and excrement in which errant pigs wallowed. Some newcomers wanted to turn back to their Northern comforts.

Tourist disenchantment was to be avoided at all costs. The aristocratic visitor with his entourage, heavy purse and readily available credit was an opportunity. He or she might keep an innkeeper, a coachman, a stablehand, a postilion, a washerwoman, a tailor if not several and many more besides in gainful employment for a significant period. If the aristocrat were particularly well-heeled, there might even be in prospect some foreign travel, a longer term stipend and occasionally even a pension. It was imperative to seize the day and ensure these precious commodities did not lose their focus.

The locals were stupefied that the newcomers gave the relatively recent additions to the city no more than a passing glance. Michelangelo's and Bernini's gate, the obelisk of Sixtus V on the Piazza del Popolo, the magnificent staircase of the Campidoglio and the steps and terraces of the Piazza di Spagna, were dismissed after quick inspection. Instead, the travellers rushed to see the ancient remains, unprepared for the sights which greeted them. They had not anticipated the ravages wrought by flood, earthquake and man. The temples, baths and amphitheatres which their privileged classical educations had led them to expect to see whole were mere fragments, plundered by Renaissance and Baroque masters to feed their art. The ancient sites were for the most part buried under rubbish and earth overgrown with weeds. The visitors found that what remained had been corrupted. The Pantheon and Baths of Diocletian had been turned into the Churches of Santa Maria ad Martyres and of Santa Maria degli Angeli, and Hadrian's tomb had been converted into the Castel Sant'Angelo. Trajan and Marcus Aurelius in Carrara marble had been supplanted by St Peter and St Paul in bronze on their respective columns.

Just as the locals were perplexed, so the new tourists were uncomprehending as regards what seemed to them the locals' seeming indifference to their ancient heritage. The typical Roman was comfortable among his ruins, his normality reflected in the horned oxen lying beside obelisks in the fora and goats grazing among broken statues nibbling at grapes pushing up through fallen marble. He expected to see finds rehabilitated in a fresh environment. The wealthiest and most illustrious in society had always collected the finest of everything, so to see mosaics, statuary and bas-reliefs lifted from ancient sites and displayed in the homes of the powerful was nothing out of the ordinary. Giovanni Battista had no qualms about travellers muddying their hands in the undergrowth and trawling through derelict buildings for souvenirs.

Antiquities were not all the wealthy foreigners planned to take home. They also wanted images of the places they had visited. One of the first artists to exploit the demand was another Giovanni Battista. Piranesi pumped out fantasised scenes which spawned a fashion which would keep artists and printers in work for centuries. But Giovanni Battista Lusieri refused to work from what he called miserable sketches created largely from the imagination. He preferred to complete his compositions on location, reproducing light and shade with far greater accuracy than had ever been seen before. His faithful, highly detailed landscapes were to take the art world by storm both on and beyond the Italian peninsula leading to his appointment to the Royal Bourbon Court of Naples.

But royal patronage did not equal the challenge represented by Lord Elgin's brief to record for posterity all previously uncharted archaeological wonders lying between the Ottoman capital, Constantinople, and Athens. According to the terms of the agreement reached, Giovanni Battista, by now affectionately known as Don Tito, would be paid a princely annual salary of two hundred pounds and all his expenses, and was tasked with hiring a team of craftsmen of his choosing. It seemed he had everything to gain and nothing to lose. A retainer by a permanent patron particularly at a time of political uncertainty, Napoleon having occupied Rome and Naples exiling the Bourbons to Palermo, seemed the stuff of dreams. From now on, Giovanni Battista would be able to devote himself exclusively to his art. Or so it seemed.

Deborah Jay worked as a reader in French and Italian for Random House and as an A-level history teacher following a career as a project finance lawyer. She recently completed a biography entitled *Marie-Louise, Napoleon's Other Wife* and is writing a fictionalised memoir of Emperor Francis I/II of Austria in addition to completing her biography of Giovanni Battista Lusieri.

GWENLLIAN JONES
Self Portrait

A glimpse of my mother through Edouard Manet's oil painting Au Bal. *Extract.*

AS I GET CLOSER, SHE TURNS AWAY FROM ME. She looks over her shoulder and out through the neo-classical window at the courtyard below. Two transvestites glide through the crowd on stilts, revelling in the glitter of flashing cameras. Stewards like statues, standing firm in pointed brown leather boots and knee-length ponchos, glaring, but watching nothing in particular. Fashionistas flaunt themselves between the clusters of onlookers and photographers, flawless and uninhibited by doubt and anxiety.

I'd worked my way through the swarm of people earlier, skirting my way along the wall and yearning to fit in, or to stand out – I hadn't been too sure. I look down on my coat again, worn stubbornly through two winters despite having neither a hood nor a warm lining. I swear to myself that it didn't look this shabby in the mirror this morning. The elastic of my jeans starts to feel slack around my knees where they've crumpled from the day's walking. I feel sluggish, below par.

My eyes return to her, but she is still distracted. I will her to turn around, but she looks on.

SELF PORTRAIT

I don't necessarily go to galleries for the art on display. I go for the space in between. When I lived in Dublin I used to go into the National Gallery on my way home from the university. Now and then, when I felt like I needed to learn something, I'd latch on to a few utterances of a guided tour as it passed. But most of the time, I would wander in my own company. I had little knowledge of any painting there to begin with – or art in general for that matter – but gradually, I began to learn how to read them. I began to build my own relationship with them. Some would stick for a while, calling me over on every visit. But others I would return to a stranger, unable to uncover what I had before – mere fleeting fancies. I would move on, leaving an image that was to my eyes both whole and utterly incomplete – menacing, as if it would come to life only when my back was turned.

Rooms in galleries are, for the most part, hollow. They are empty; the furniture has been taken out, and with them, the purpose they once held. In darkness, devoid of people and still, they are little more than abandoned hallways. The hangings on the walls are silent, muted along with their past. But as I walked around, the setting sun igniting the feather-fall of dust in its beam, the sound of my step reverberated through all the things that linger in the gap between the frames.

In daytime, the place is filled with people; their lives, their thoughts and their contemplations. The paintings, in their turn, are privy to all these feelings. Facing each other over a vacuum, cut off from those around them, they are often met with meddling eyes; people searching for significance, meanings, truths. They might not care what we feel, or what we see. But they will tolerate everyone in their turn. They exist as objects of admiration to the trained eye, but also of reflection. The chasm between the image and the onlooker becomes a myriad of experience with each new glance offering a new understanding, weaving into it a new outcome.

The Courtauld Gallery wasn't busy. Most of the clatter had been absorbed by the opening weekend of London Fashion Week in the courtyard outside, the noise amplifying the emptiness on the second floor. I stepped into the Impressionists room and saw a woman sitting on the wooden bench in front of Manet's *A Bar at the Folies-Bergère*. I hovered by her side a while as she examined the image in front of us. I recognised the picture of a jigsaw I'd helped my dad with some years ago. Mam would always get him a new one at Christmas and he'd sit for hours every evening, studying every morsel in front of him. Sometimes, he wouldn't even think to take off his suit jacket.

I remember thinking that the picture was a strange choice. She looked miserable, and I wondered why anyone would want to paint someone who looked so sad. The image of the man in the mirror wasn't done very well, I said to him one night as I examined the lid of the box. But Dad was tired, and it wasn't up for discussion. Could I see a piece that looked like it could be part of a tangerine?

As I made my way under the doorframe to the next room, now home to Van Gogh and Edouard Manet, I realised how much comfort I felt in the steady echo of my footsteps as they followed me in. When I saw her she was standing over to the corner of the room. The lower half of her evening dress cut off by the frame, the rest of her only hinting at her person. The colour of her flesh was still there, but her limbs were out of sight, suspended in a place beyond the wooden pane. Her hair was tied up by a clip – a single, bold brushstroke – and brushed behind an ear that was no more than two thin flicks of dark paint.

Unlike the other faces I have already passed, she is different. The eighteenth-century nobles on the previous floor had been immortalised in their wealth, their gaze fixed so confidently on whoever stood before them that you'd almost be sure they were looking back. Their costumes were impeccably drawn, and a careful pose – the pursing of lips, the deliberate placement of hands – left no doubt about their perceived power and importance. Name, persona, reputation – all determined, unblemished by subjective interpretation.

Manet had given her proportion, but the rest of her features are left only roughly defined. A whisper of an eyelid grazes the space above her nose, her body shape tucked tightly under her dress. The colours on her dress have started to run, too, and she almost looks like she's trying to melt away from the frame, to be set free to walk amongst the crowd below.

At first I thought that she might've been turning away from him, like someone who doesn't like having their photo taken would turn away from a camera. After all, who was Manet to try to pen her down? Or to contain her multitudes in one snapshot, adorned in a ball gown and prim as a picture? She seemed defiant rather than shy, not one to put on a show when there was nothing to say. I admired her for a while.

But now I'm starting to take it personally. I'm urging her to turn around and look at me, so I can see her. I want her to show herself to me as she is. The longer I think, the more I speculate, interrupting her story with my own version of it. She allows for my intrusion, though she doesn't seem to acknowledge it. I find myself uncovering her eyes with my own, placing them where they should be and fighting with the plain fact that they are not there. I imagine the slow curve of her head as she turns to face me, but what I visualise doesn't quite fit. And as soon as it comes, it dissipates into a thousand dots in front of my eyes and she is looking out the window again. Stubbornly.

When I was twenty, I decided that I needed to give my fringe another go. I had one up until I was six when I swiftly decided that I was too old for it – they really weren't for grown-ups. I then spent the next year growing it out, much to the despair of my mother who had to force me into tight plastic hairbands every morning to keep the thick tuft out of my eyes.

I arrived back at my flat feeling renewed, rushing to the bathroom mirror to inspect my new look. My eyes lingered for a long time, adjusting themselves to the new reflection and seeing another's more clearly than they had for a long time. My reaction was the same as that of the people at home when I saw them the following summer. Dad didn't say much at first, but he eventually managed a 'very nice' when I pressed him for a reaction, just like Mam used to have to do.

It still happens sometimes. '...Gwenllian?' they ask. I nod and smile, knowing what's to follow. 'For a second I thought I saw your mother there!' they say, and I feel guilty for a second, thinking that I've deceived them somehow.

When I was growing up, people would always comment on how similar we were, but we never really saw it. We discussed it in the car on the way home from getting the paper. *Do you see it?* She would ask. No, not at all. *Probably for the best.* But there she was, years later, in the mirror of my Temple Bar flat in Dublin.

I have few pictures of her. She didn't like to be photographed. I have one that was taken of her paragliding in France. She's looking up at the lens, and she's smiling. Not for the photograph, but because she's happy. I was too young to join her up there at the time, but I've done it since. I tried to replicate the picture myself, as if I'd be able to show it to her one day. But my eyes are squinting from the sun's glare and my smile is unconvincing, clearly terrified of dropping the camera to the lake below. Only hers made it onto the wall.

When I first looked at Manet's portrait, I told myself I was seeing my mother. The smudged features like the gradual retreat of her face from my memory. The part of her that others saw in me, I could – for a while – throw onto the canvas in front of my eyes. There she was; turning away, refusing to look me in the eye in case I might think that she was really there. Her hidden expression resonated in me the countless times I have tried to conjure her image in my mind, and failed. Or the times I have strained to hear her voice, and instead only managing a passing remark – distant, as if she was already halfway through the door.

The tone is still there if I dig deep enough for it; but the pattern, the melody of her accent, had disappeared – the muddle of *gog* and *hwntw*, north and south. I heard it on a holiday tape a little while ago. It was taken on a holiday in Majorca in 1994. We were having dinner at a restaurant and she asked me to stand on the plastic chair to sing a nursery rhyme. 'C'mon' she said, encouraging me, whispering along to the first line. 'Adeiladu ty bach, un, dau, tri...' But I didn't recognise her voice.

But, looking at it again, I realise that it is me. What I'm seeing is my own desire to rid her from my body. Not to free myself of her – and certainly not to forget her – but to release her from my futile grasp, so she might stop running away. I've long given her a voice to replace the one that's lost, and the words to say when I ask and she refuses to answer. I have been recklessly smoothing over the gaps, and she has become almost irretrievable.

    I follow her gaze once more to the courtyard. I look down again at my jeans and walk, diligently, to the next painting.

Gwenllian Jones, originally from Snowdonia, moved to Ireland in order to read History and English Literature at Trinity College, Dublin. A keen traveller, she then went to South America before coming to Norwich to study her MA. A native Welsh speaker, her writing is often concerned with questions of identity.

LESLENE KWAME

The Wild Card of Antarctica

An extract from a work in progress

I TIS NEW YEAR'S EVE, 1910.
 The bow of The Terra Nova ploughs slowly through the Antarctic's Ross Sea as floes impede the heavily-laden ship. A snowstorm earlier in the day makes the deck feel cold and damp as chunks of melting ice fall from the ship's ropes like ripe fruits from a tree. Though it is summertime, awe-inspiring mountains of frozen water pose as abstract sculptures in the perilous sea. Captain Robert Falcon Scott and his crew are within two days' sail of Ross Island, the final destination from which the march to the South Pole will begin. In the distance Mount Sabine illuminated by the midnight sun evokes a vision of purity that leaves Dr Edward Leicester Atkinson Junior, the ship's surgeon, contemplative. He thinks to share the sight with the youngest member of the wardroom, Aspley Cherry-Garrard.
 'Wrap a blanket around you Cherry and come up on deck,' says Atkinson trying to rouse the sleeping man. Captain Scott and most of the crew have already retired to bed. The last twenty-four hours had been difficult.
 'Have you seen the land?' Atkinson says in an attempt to motivate Cherry to leave the warmth of his bunk. Cherry protests but lets himself be persuaded.
 Up on deck Cherry is captivated by the magnificence of the sight and will later write in his 1922 memoir *The Worst Journey in the World*, 'They were the most glorious peaks appearing as it were like satin.'
 The cold gets the better of Cherry who abandons Atkinson on deck. But it's not just the sunlight and the landscape that enchant

THE WILD CARD OF ANTARCTICA

Atkinson; marking the beginning of the New Year is a religious ritual that he always observes. It reminds him too of a childhood of which he barely speaks.

*

The Forest School dormitory that Atkinson shared with five other teenaged boys was especially cold that night in December 1895. His feet felt as if they had been covered with ground frost. Sleep evaded him. From his bed, the horizon of leafless trees that once proudly displayed plumes of greens, yellows and golden browns, appeared emaciated, raising bony outstretched limbs towards an indifferent sky.

Three silhouettes invaded the moonlit room. Before he could clearly determine what loomed over him, the covers were pulled from his diminutive frame. He found himself being frogmarched along the near-freezing corridors into blackness and utter confusion. In the dark, a rope tightened around his waist. As one former Forest Boy recalled in his memoir: 'The Blackdrop was a horrible and unforgettable experience that happened at least once to every new boy.' The 'Blackdrop' was a gap in the top of the attic stairwell that created a drop of several flights of stairs to the ground floor. When the lights went out, the new boy would be lowered by rope into the dark crevice, and if he screamed, the drop would be repeated.

The boys plunged Atkinson into the pitch black.

*

Atkinson's father, Edward Leicester Atkinson, knew all about boarding schools and their initiation pranks having spent more than ten years of his life at them. He had primed his son to expect nothing less than bullying and hardship – an evil he considered necessary if his son was to have the character of an Englishman and gentleman.

Edward's mother died in 1860 when he was nine years old, leaving him and his older brother with an ambitious father, the Canon J C Atkinson, who in 1847 became the first vicar in Danby, an ancient village in Cleveland, Yorkshire. The Canon was a strict disciplinarian who also had a reputation for being a social climber among those who knew him best. When he remarried two years after his wife's death, Edward was sent to Rosall School in Lancashire and from there to Repton in Derby. Denied the opportunity to experience a stable, loving family, Edward's formative years were shaped by the prevailing ethos of public school education: harsh discipline and imperialist ideologies. By the time he decided against continuing his education to university, the Canon, his father, had remarried twice and sired eleven more children.

Barely twenty-one, in 1871 Edward joined the Colonial Bank in Bishopsgate, London as an accounts clerk. Within eighteen months of his appointment he was transferred to their branch in Barbados and then to St Vincent. It was while posted in St Vincent that he met and married Jane Ann Hazell, a fifth-generation white Creole. They immediately started a family. Edward was determined to be a devoted husband and father. His seven daughters and one son, Atkinson Junior, were born all over what was then the British West Indies.

After twenty-four years' service Edward was still without the position he most desired, the General Manager of the Port-of-Spain branch of the Colonial Bank in Trinidad. The problems of the post-emancipation economy of the late nineteenth century had forced large numbers of well-to-do whites to abandon the West Indies, creating a vacuum that was being filled by a rising number of non-whites. This trend bothered Edward, who believed in the superiority of the English and rejected ideas of power-sharing with people he thought had their place elsewhere in society. Edward's imperialist ideologies and prejudices hastened his plans for his fourteen-year-old son, whose exposure even to white Creole society had been curtailed. Atkinson Junior had been home-schooled up to the point of his admission to Forest School at Snaresbrook, London in October 1895.

*

Forest School during Atkinson's time enjoyed a prestige generally reserved for public schools. It had royal patronage, the endorsement of the Bishop of Colchester and participated in cadet and sporting events with students from Eton, Rugby, Winchester, Harrow and the other five schools identified by the 1868 Public Schools Act. The Headmaster, Reverend Ralph C Guy, a twenty-eight-year-old Oxford graduate, assumed headship of Forest School in 1894. R C Guy, who had all the right connections to the best of English society, set about grooming his students after the fashions and traditions of the leading public schools. Atkinson's ideas about Empire and England, first fostered by his father, flourished at the school. It also gave him an appetite for hardiness and competition.

*

As one of the eight thousand hopefuls who responded to the Royal Geographical Society's advert in *The Times* newspaper on 13th September 1909, the odds of Atkinson being included among the seven naval officers who would accompany Captain Scott on his expedition to the South Pole were as high as finding a snowball in the tropics – and Atkinson knew it. That knowledge did not dissuade him from applying, and he eventually succeeded in being appointed the ship's surgeon. He capitalised on that access to the Antarctic to explore and discover new life forms. In a press interview in New Zealand in October 1910 he told reporters, 'It was a voyage of scientific discoveries,' hinting at why the Terra Nova Expedition was important to him. It was to be his research in Antarctica that helped to build his reputation as a scientist and parasitologist.

On the 12th October 1910 a telegram awaited Captain Scott and his crew. Roald Amundsen, the Norwegian explorer, had misled Scott as to his true intentions and was in a competing race to the South Pole. The news was met with mixed reactions. Atkinson was buoyed up by the competition. He welcomed the opportunity to reinforce the dominance of the British Empire and to be part of what he naturally assumed would be the winning team.

*

After the 'Blackdrop' on that cold December night of 1895, Atkinson began swimming in the school's outdoor pool. Reconciled to the fact that he would never be warm again, he cared not that the pool was unheated. He was set on overcoming what he perceived to be his disadvantages. According to Forest School journals, in July 1896 Atkinson got his first mention in their newsletter for winning a swimming race. A mention was like a public pat on the back and every Forest boy wanted it. It was also unashamedly biased towards achievers and encouraged fierce competition amongst the boys. Forest School's 150th Anniversary Commemoration Book notes: 'The cult of Muscular Christianity which swept through public schools finally descended upon Forest and R C Guy would appear to be its High Priest.'

If Guy was its high priest, then Atkinson was the altar boy, for he began winning nearly every sporting competition in the school. He became Forest's Boxing Champion, won several medals for swimming, track and field, and was an adept footballer. Once he had established himself as a valued member of the student body, his social abilities and leadership skills began to bloom although he was still considered 'quiet'. He also gained recognition in his academic work, winning prizes for chemistry and mathematics. After graduating from Forest, he continued his sporting achievements at St Thomas Medical School. It was evident that Atkinson enjoyed winning.

*

It is 4th January 1911, 6:00am.

Captain Scott, Lieutenant Edward Evans and Dr Edward Wilson disembark: they are leaving the ship to identify a suitable camp site. The animals have had a difficult forty-eight hours and the seventeen ponies are particularly restless. Captain Oates, whose primary responsibility is the care of the ponies, tries to settle them, while Atkinson assists. Atkinson notices that Scott and his team return much sooner than expected. They are in jubilant mood as Scott informs the crew that the campsite is much nearer than initially thought and he has christened it 'Cape Evans' after his second in command, Lieutenant Evans.

THE WILD CARD OF ANTARCTICA

Dr Edward Leicester Atkinson cannot imagine as he steps on to the vast landscape of whiteness that within fifteen months, he, the lowest ranking naval officer, will assume command of the Expedition. As he helps to offload the equipment and animals from the Terra Nova he cannot imagine that it will be he who receives the news that Amundsen beat Scott in the race to the Pole. Or that in November 1912 it will be he who will lead the search for the bodies of Scott, Bowers, Wilson, Oates and Evans, the party that will march to the South Pole a few months later, and that history will accuse him of causing their deaths. Such things are inconceivable in the festive atmosphere. The sun is high in the turquoise sky, the sounds of men's laughter and excitement echo, the ponies and the sleigh dogs roll playfully on the snow-covered beach, as colonies of penguins squawk and waddle while schools of whales enjoy the melting waters. It is a wonderful summer's day on Ross Island.

Leslene Kwame's non-fiction projects include the story of the Antarctic explorer Dr Edward L Atkinson and a biography of the Ghanaian economist and central banker John S Addo who served his country during its most turbulent political period. She also writes crime and historical fiction.

AMY McTIGHE

Anfal

Threatened by Saddam Hussein's chemical bombs, a Kurdish family is forced to embark on a perilous journey.

August 25th 1988, Barwari, Iraqi Kurdistan

THE ORDER ARRIVED ONE NIGHT IN LATE SUMMER. A messenger from the Peshmerga came down from the mountains and crept from house to house with instructions from the families' husbands and fathers.

They are coming for you.
You must get out. Now. Get out and go far.
Keep walking north until you get to Turkey.
We will find you.
Don't worry.
Everything will be OK.

Lazheen lit just enough candles for the family to see and told her two older children to pack what clothes they could fit into a small bag. Kerzen, only four, slept on. In the half light Lazheen stuffed nuts and apples and cheese into a bag and some old, treasured photographs into her pocket. She woke Kerzen, who protested loudly, and dressed her in clothes far too warm for the August night, telling the others to do the same.

Lazheen's mother-in-law Yasna gathered her few belongings in a brief, practised move and began to prepare breakfast for them all. She mixed flour and water, then went into the yard behind their one-room mud-brick house and squatted beside the clay-lined pit filled with embers from last night's fire. She worked small pieces of the dough into large, thin circles and then spread them one by one over a metal dome in the pit. Her eldest granddaughter, Sipel, joined her and in the moonlight they silently baked thirty thin flatbreads, folding the finished discs, bubbling and cracking, into a bag.

When all of their preparations were complete, the family sat on foam mats around the edge of the room. Yasna and Lazheen drank hot, sweet tea in silence as the children shared a can of Coca-Cola. An indignant yelp by Sipel was quickly stifled. Her brother Darra had spat in the can and Sipel refused to drink it. She began to cry. Lazheen gave her a piece of bread and Darra a perfunctory slap.

'How will we know where to go?' asked Lazheen.

'They will send us guides, don't worry,' replied Yasna.

'I'll carry the bags if you carry Kerzen when she gets tired.'

'Of course,' said Yasna, stroking the little girl's head.

'We mustn't get split up – Ibrahim has to be able to find us when we get to Turkey.'

'It will be OK Lazheen. Now take some rest.'

Lazheen lay down, but couldn't sleep. She listened hard for the sound of engines.

Baghdad, Eighteen Months Earlier

The Kurds of the north of Iraq were an indefatigable source of aggravation for leaders of modern-day Mesopotamia; from the Ottoman Empire through to the Second American War in 2003. The Ba'ath Party had been lenient when it first took power in 1968 and designated a 'Kurdish Autonomous Region' from the early 1970s. But the Kurds were not content with what they saw as superficial rights and continued repression of a substantive role in the running of their own territory and people.

The Kurdish Peshmerga rebels – called 'saboteurs' by the Iraqi government – conducted regular attacks on Iraqi government and army installations for decades, but it was their intermittent tactical support for Iran during the Iran-Iraq war of 1980-1988 that most provoked Iraqi President and leader of the Ba'ath Party, Saddam Hussein. Iraq needed a final solution to the Kurdish problem.

```
The Revolutionary Command Council decided in its meeting on
29th March 1987 the following:

First: The Comrade Ali Hassan Al-Majid... will represent the
Regional Command of the Party and the Revolutionary Command
Council in implementing their policies in all of the northern
region, including the Autonomous Region of Kurdistan, in order
to protect security and order and guarantee stability and the
implementation of the Autonomy Law in the region.

Second: The Comrade... will have authority over all the state's
civil, military and security apparatuses to carry out this decree.

Saddam Hussein
President of the Revolutionary Command Council
```

Al-Majid, Hussein's cousin, was notoriously brutal. A former *mustashar* (advisor) once commented that 'In tough cases, in which [Hussein] needs people without a heart, he calls upon Ali Hassan Al-Majid'. His campaign against the Kurds was given the codename 'Anfal', meaning 'spoils of war', from a passage in the Koran about wars between 'believers' and 'unbelievers', and the former's entitlement to looted bounty. Its relevance was marginal but the use of archaic religious references as codenames was common practice – pre-emptive justification of the Ba'ath Party's actions, and assertion of their right to act on behalf of the people of an ancient nation.

The Iraqi army had found fighting the Peshmerga in their native, mountainous territory a near-impossible task. Al-Majid's first move was to turn his attention to their civilian support. He knew that the villagers of rural Kurdistan were providing food, clothing, medical assistance and other resources to the Peshmerga and without them the rebels would struggle to survive. A programme of village 'collectivisation' soon followed. Vast swathes of Kurdistan – anywhere further than 5km from a major population centre or highway – were designated out of bounds on the grounds that the Iraqi army couldn't guarantee their security. Residents of these villages were relocated to *mujamma'at*; large, high-security camps, and their homes were razed to the ground. Al-Majid ordered that if any armed resistance was encountered during this process, the entire village was to be killed in reprisal.

Over the next two years, slowed only by a squeeze on military resources because of the war with Iran, village collectivisation was enforced ever deeper into Peshmerga territory and closer to the borders with Iran and Turkey. Al-Majid also rolled out more regular use of his new military tool: chemical bombs.

Al-Majid had crossed the chemical threshold within weeks of his appointment. In April 1987 a key Peshmerga leader (and now President of Iraq) Jalal Talabani asked to open a channel of communication with Al-Majid. Al-Majid's response was to drop chemical bombs on Talabani's headquarters and the surrounding area. Discussing this attack in a meeting later, Al-Majid was recorded as saying (of the Kurdish villagers who wanted to stay in their homes across Kurdistan) 'I will kill them all with chemical weapons! Who is going to say anything? The international community? Fuck them!'

The use of chemical bombs began in earnest in spring 1988 in a campaign that lasted until September of that year. Barwari, the fertile mountainous region in the far north-west of Kurdistan, was one of his final targets. Pockmarked with caves into which villagers scattered when their villages were attacked by Iraqi war planes, it was proving hard to bring the region to heel. In late August 1988 the Peshmerga, who now stayed well away from their villages for fear of bringing reprisal attacks on their families, heard that chemical bombs had been dropped on a village in the region. It had started. The Peshmerga leadership sent messengers as fast as possible to the villages, telling them that they had to flee. Their only hope was to get to the Turkish border, several days' walk away, and pray that they would be allowed in. The men of the Peshmerga were powerless to help their wives, mothers and children, who would have to fend for themselves in the wilderness of the high mountains.

AMY MCTIGHE

August 25th 1988, Barwari, Kurdistan

The first cockerels began to crow. Lazheen and Yasna rolled out their prayer mats to face Mecca as the children rested, fully dressed, under pungent sheepskins. After her usual recitations Lazheen stayed prostrate for a few moments extra. She prayed to God that she would be able to protect her children, that the chemical bombs would not find them, that they would survive the journey through the harsh mountains and that the Turks would allow them in. She prayed that Ibrahim would not be killed and that he would find them again.

Then Lazheen and Yasna woke the children and went out into the cool of the early morning. In the watery light of dawn they saw a procession of families walking quickly and silently out of the village. The line of people stretched past the houses and through the orchards, scented and heavy with apples, reaching steadily upwards until the track thinned to a goat-herding path, finally disappearing into the mist hanging low on the rocky outcrops above.

This is an edited extract of a book on the flight of Iraqi Kurdish villagers in 1988 from the chemical bombardments of Saddam Hussein's Anfal campaign. It follows one woman and her family as they walk for five days and nights through the treacherous mountains of northern Iraq to Turkey, pursued by the Iraqi army.

All Kurdish names have been changed. The translations of Ba'ath Party documents and meeting recordings were taken from Genocide in Iraq: The Anfal Campaign Against the Kurds, *published in 1993 by Human Rights Watch.*

Amy McTighe has been a Foreign and Commonwealth Office diplomat, English teacher, archaeologist and journalist. She speaks Arabic and has lived and worked across Africa and the Middle East. She writes fiction and non-fiction and has reported for *The Times*. She now splits her time between Norwich and the volcanic island of Montserrat.

PETER NOBLE

TRUTH

Reflections following an endurance event, for which any talent was shattered long ago. And how.

'I'M NOT AN ATHLETE.' I wrote that sitting on the Eurostar, travelling back to London from Paris. Legs tingling, heavy with exhaustion; arse feeling every click, clack, clickety-clack in the firmness of the standard class seat cushion; hand shaking as I wrote the words. We'd cycled 320 miles in four days to get there, exposed bits covered in lotion one day, under sunshine that frizzled your skin while you watched; or hidden in reflective waterproofs the next, bright yellows and oranges shining through rain that coagulated into a single sheet, hiding us from one another as we navigated our amphibious a-frames blindly through the downpour. Two hours to get back.

*

I was twelve years old and an odd, hippie boy when I ended up at the London Nautical (school number fourteen of eighteen). I'd been to India and to public school. I didn't know what my eleven-plus score had been because I'd done Common Entrance a year early. So I dropped my aitches and slung my brown Adidas sports bag over my shoulder, keeping it in place with one hand and studied nonchalance – but I was still relegated to the fringes of the pack in the tyranny of the playground.

TRUTH

Thomas West lived on a barge – which I thought was probably cool, and served to explain why he was at a nautical school – but eccentricity was unacceptable in that unfathomable hierarchy of small boys. Unusually for a state school, our naval battledress uniforms were tailored, with brass buttons and cap badge. But West's uniform was clearly second-hand and hung shapelessly on him, discoloured from washing where ours were dry-cleaned and pressed. Someone found out that West's middle name was Melvyn. Given the state of his uniform, this naturally became 'Smellvyn'. In the way of boys on the fringe, I tried to insinuate myself into the pack by joining in the alienation of a fellow outcast.

'Oi! Smellvyn!' I shouted.

West turned on me with an accumulated ferocity that he could only direct at the weakest pack member. He growled with the frustration of insults collected, compressed and packed away in hidden places, and leapt at me with both fists. The playground full of boys gathered in a joyful throng as we prepared to pummel each other into the dust.

'Fight! Fight! Fight!' The throng was delighted at the prospect of a freak show.

I twisted backwards, hardly feeling West's lunge as his fist glanced off my left shoulder. I lost my balance as I turned, and we both fell. I was still turning, and West's momentum pulled him round, hitting the ground first in the rolling movement. As I pulled myself up, I threw all my weight into an uncontrolled punch that bounced West's head off the tarmac. That was it. We stood up, blinking, looking at each other. It was over. The mob drifted away, as boys searched for the next entertainment.

I'd been hazed at boarding school: apple-pie bedding was an entrance ritual. I'd been mercilessly punished at the Gordon Schools in Huntly, because of my English accent. (I never did persuade them that my father's family was from Aberdeenshire.) I'd never been in a fight. I'd never punched another boy, or been punched in anger. I didn't enjoy it.

My mother assessed the damage that evening. I'd punched nothing tougher than a really hard pillow before, and lack of technique meant that my hand had swelled up like a plumped cushion, my knuckles now puffy indentations. There was no way I could hold a pen. It was a Wednesday evening in early July, exams were finished, and school was preparing to break up for the long summer holiday.

'No. You can't stay home from school tomorrow. I don't care if you can't write – you shouldn't have been fighting. You can still *hear* the teachers,' said my mother.

*

I looked up at the kitchen clock that Thursday morning, cramming wholegrain Shreddies and goat's milk into my mouth but holding the spoon in my left hand, cradling against my chest the plumped cushion that my right had become after the punch. I was late for the train to Waterloo. The London Nautical School operated a naval regime: timekeeping was paramount. Prefects would stand at the side entrance barrier in Stamford Street and place latecomers on the 'defaulters' list: detention. A couple of weeks away from the end of the school year, summer poking highlights round the corner, and defaulters would be a crap way to end the week.

I plonked my naval cap on my head, its removable white cover greyed by the London air, but still smart with its brass badge. I'd change the cloth cover over the summer. I picked up my brown Adidas sports bag with my left hand and flung it over my shoulder, ran down the passage from the kitchen to the front door – two skips to the right through the s-bend at the bottom of the stairs – and tucked the bag under my chin to free up that left hand so I could open the front door.

I pulled the door closed behind me and stepped through the front gate onto the pavement. I don't remember anything else. I've pieced the next month together from stories.

I ran down to the corner, over Broughton Street to the traffic lights outside Brewer's the newsagents. This was where I always crossed the busy main road. I poked my head out behind a white van parked at the kerb, to check the traffic. Clear, so I ran across. A man on the other pavement was waving at me, shouting at me to get back. The Citroën DS coming from the other direction braked as he saw me.

I thought the Citroën DS was cool: I loved the space-age body shape and the single-spoke steering wheel.

TRUTH

Police measurements of the skid length indicated that the driver was going through a green light at 32 mph. It wasn't his fault, but the car tore open my left thigh and flung my slight, twelve-year-old body through the air. I flew at a height of about six feet and travelled 20 feet up Queenstown Road, landing on my head next to a storm drain.

Ed and my mother came out of the house together. Ed would drop my mother at her office and then drive on to his own. They noticed the commotion at the traffic light.

My mother saw the white naval cap.

In the evenings after work, my mother was reading *Power in Praise* by Merlin Carothers (1974). The message was simple: praise God in all situations, because all things work together for good. All things.

Including finding your small boy in a bloody heap as you leave for work in the morning.

All things.

'Praise the Lord, praise the Lord,' my mother muttered as she ran towards the gathered crowd.

'Praise the Lord, praise the Lord,' my mother muttered, as she knelt next to me and waited for the ambulance.

'Praise the Lord, praise the Lord,' my mother muttered, a mantra as she travelled with me under blue lights to the hospital.

My mother is a literal woman.

*

The ambulance took me to St Thomas's Hospital on the South Bank of the Thames. I was assessed and transferred to the Gough-Cooper Department of Neurological Surgery, then at the National Hospital for Nervous Diseases, Maida Vale.

The right side of my skull was fractured. My right eye was bleeding, bruised and swollen. My left side was paralysed, so the muscles of the left side of my face had stopped working, my cheeks sagged and my mouth drooped to the left. I had no control of my left arm or leg. But it hurt.

There was bleeding inside my skull and around my brain, but no specific damage so they didn't need to operate. And, on the plus side, it hurt. A lot. Which meant the paralysis wasn't from a spinal injury.

In 1974, two professors from the University of Glasgow's Institute of Neurological Sciences, Graham Teasdale and Bryan J Jennett, published the Glasgow Coma Scale. It's called the GCS in Medspeak. A patient is assessed against the three criteria of the scale, scoring from one to five, and given a cumulative score between three (deep coma) and fifteen (fully awake). Generally a score below nine indicates a severe injury. Eye opening in response to pain but not speech gives a score of two; making incomprehensible sounds gives a score of two; extensor motor response gives a score of two. That would be a combined GCS score of six.

Thinking out loud in front of my mother, the medical team discussed the question of surgery, so she prayed. She sat in a waiting room, praying. She prayed until an internal voice told her it was all going to be OK. But the computerised tomography (Medspeak: CT or CAT) scans showed no specific injury to my brain and there was no need to operate. My mother has relayed this exchange to me as evidence of the power of prayer: 'The doctors were going to operate, but I prayed. And they came back in and said they didn't need to.'

As a miracle, it fell short of a full cure. The power of prayer palliative was enough only to mitigate injuries. Had the medical team been more circumspect in their discussions, this impressionable tree-hugger, wrestling Christian Science ('None of it's real, it's all Error') against a newfound fundamental, born-again Christianity ('God will heal your child if you have enough faith'), might have taken on more responsibility for her son's recovery. Instead of leaning back on the self-soothing comfort of magical thinking.

Another measure of the severity of traumatic brain injury (Medspeak: TBI) is post-traumatic amnesia (Medspeak: PTA). This is a state of ambulatory unconsciousness and random, sometimes bizarre behaviour. Three and a half weeks is pretty damned severe. I have no memory of the rest of July.

I have no memory of standing on my bed, looking out at the Thames and saying, 'I don't like this boat.'

TRUTH

I have no memory of space flights, or cravings for fish and chips.

I have no memory of wanderings round the hospital, family at a safe distance behind to make sure I didn't get myself into any more trouble.

I have no memory of asking my mother where my other four legs were, because I was a quinx and I should have six. And no, I don't know what a quinx is either.

Continuous memory came back on the day I was discharged. Hospital radio played Amii Stewart singing *Knock on Wood*. I tried to play table tennis in the ward's recreation area but I couldn't close my left hand around the ball. I couldn't throw it in the air to hit it with the bat, or even pick it up off the table. I sat in the book area and tried to read, but the letters on the page swam about like oddly shaped fish.

We didn't have a car any more – Ed had given up his job to take care of me, and it had been a perk – so we walked from the hospital to catch the bus home. I tried to leapfrog a bollard in the road, but I jumped straight into it.

I slept in my bed, and in the morning I told my mother and Ed about a bad dream I'd had, where I'd been in an accident and I'd been in hospital.

'It wasn't a dream,' they told me.

'Oh,' I said, and went to brush my teeth.

I slept in my bed, but in the middle of the night I tried to climb into my mother's wardrobe because it was a spaceship. My mother steered me gently towards the shuttle in my bedroom, and back to sleep.

*

Life crashes into you and you are ambushed by events. I also wrote that on the Eurostar.

Peter Noble is an actor and a singer. A regular on London's spoken word scene reading other people's writing, his own project tells of long-distance cycle rides: charity events prompted by the death of his daughter, undertaken without ability, with insufficient training and a marked tendency towards unnecessary physical damage.

CHARLOTTE PEACOCK
The Road to Knowledge

Searching for Nan Shepherd (1893-1981)

I HAVE NEVER CLIMBED A MOUNTAIN. Nor have I ever had the slightest desire to. It is no coincidence that I live in the flatlands of Suffolk. I have been to Scotland numerous times, but I have never seen the Cairngorms, except in photographs. Then I read Nan Shepherd's *The Living Mountain*. Then I reread it and continue to do so. On each rereading, I find something surprising, some new perspective. Something which makes me gasp and pause. I bore anyone who will listen by reading passages aloud. Take this one, for example:

'By so simple a matter, too, as altering the position of one's head, a different kind of world may be made to appear. Lay the head down, or better still, face away from what you look at, and bend with straddled legs till you see your world upside down. How new it has become! From the close-by sprigs of heather to the most distant fold of the land, each detail stands erect in its own validity. In no other way have I seen of my own unaided sight that the earth is round. As I watch, it arches its back, and each layer of landscape bristles – though bristles is a word of too much commotion for it. Details are no longer part of a grouping in a picture of which I am the focal point, the focal point is everywhere. Nothing has reference to me, the looker. This is how the earth must see itself.'

THE ROAD TO KNOWLEDGE

I would like to say, as Robert Macfarlane does in his introduction to the 2011 edition of the novella, that I read *The Living Mountain* and was changed. But that would not be the truth, exactly. The truth is, I read it and was intrigued. Not by the Cairngorms, but by the woman who wrote about them. By the woman who turned herself upside down and saw the earth as it must see itself, arching its back and bristling. Yes, I admit, I have tried it too. I will also admit to a bit of a crush on Nan Shepherd.

Any respectable work on life writing counsels the author against becoming too passionate about a potential biographical subject. After all, how can the writer remain objective and gain the reader's trust in their judgement if he or she is so in love with their subject they can see no faults? Instead, the writer is advised to maintain a healthy respect and curiosity for the subject, to balance 'empathy and detachment'. Trying to bear this in mind I found, however, that I was propelled by Shepherd's own words. In her foreword to *The Living Mountain* she writes, 'love pursued with fervour is one of the roads to knowledge.' And so it was with fervour that I began my passionate pursuit. I found her extremely elusive.

Despite the fact that Shepherd is currently enjoying something of a renaissance (all four of her prose works and her poetry anthology have recently been republished), biographical information about her is scanty. What little I could find raised more questions than it answered. My curiosity well and truly piqued, I assembled the biographical bones:

Anna 'Nan' Shepherd was born on 11 February 1893 to John and Jane Shepherd in Westerton Cottage, East Peterculter, Near Aberdeen. A month after her birth, the family moved to Dunvegan, 503 North Deeside Road in the village of Cults (pronounced 'Coolts') 3 miles west of Aberdeen, where Shepherd was to live for most of her life. Educated at the local primary school, followed by Aberdeen High School for Girls, she went on to study at the University of Aberdeen, graduating with an MA in 1915. From then on she lectured in English at the Aberdeen Training Centre for Teachers (later Aberdeen College of Education). She retired in 1956 but continued to work, editing the Aberdeen University Review until 1963. Shepherd was also a writer: during her lifetime she published four prose works and a volume of poetry.

In 1964 she was awarded an honorary doctorate by the University of Aberdeen. She died on 27 February 1981, aged eighty-eight.

There it was then: a life in one paragraph. The biographical bones needed flesh even if I were only to end up with a 'shilling life'. I assembled a chronology and a cast of characters and found I had a straightforward cradle to grave outline. But I needed more; I needed the narrative strands to weave a plot. Claire Tomalin maintains that 'what you look for when you are thinking about a biography are the stories in somebody's life.' I began to search for the stories.

In the 1930s, Anna 'Nan' Shepherd was hailed as a writer of genius. A highly respected member of the Scottish Modernist Movement, the poet, novelist and essayist was one of Scotland's best-known literati. Yet by the 1970s, she had all but been forgotten. 'That's what you call a passing reputation,' shrugged Shepherd in an interview in 1976, a twinkle in her eye.

While still in her thirties, Shepherd published three novels in quick succession. Her first, *The Quarry Wood* (1928), was praised by Hugh Walpole as 'a real addition to English Literature' for its poetic descriptions of nature. *The Weatherhouse* (1930) and *A Pass in the Grampians* (1933) were swiftly succeeded by the publication of a volume of poetry, *In the Cairngorms*, in 1934. This initial burst of activity, however, was followed by silence. Shepherd produced nothing more until 1977, when she published arguably her finest work, *The Living Mountain*.

Why the forty-year silence? When asked the question in that 1976 interview, Shepherd's answer was: 'It just didn't come to me anymore.' Yet she was still writing poetry as late as 1950. Hugh MacPherson describes three of her unpublished poems contained in a manuscript notebook at the National Library of Scotland as the best of her poetry he has seen. Moreover, articles of Shepherd's were printed in the *Aberdeen University Review* and *The Deeside Field* and her short stories appeared in *The Scots Magazine* well into her retirement from teaching.

I have my own theories about her literary silence, one of which is that this 'writer of genius gave up' because *The Living Mountain* was originally turned down for publication. Of all her works, this was the one of which Shepherd was most proud. According to her friend and fellow writer Jessie Kesson, 'she was radiant about that book and quite rightly so.' Written in the latter half of the Second World War, the manuscript was sent to one publisher who, according to Shepherd, 'politely rejected it'. She consigned the work to a drawer.

Fast-forward forty years and, as an old woman, Shepherd says she was tidying out her possessions when she came across the manuscript. Reading it again, she realised that the 'tale of her traffic with a mountain was as valid today as it was then.' Exactly why it had been rejected by the publisher during World War II, at a time when this kind of nature writing was so popular in Britain, currently mystifies me. Nevertheless, in 1977, *The Living Mountain* finally achieved publication and is now regarded as 'one of the finest books ever written on nature and landscape in Britain.'

Most works of mountaineering literature are written by men and most of these focus on the summit. Seeing one's peak is like seeing one's existence, apparently. Not for Shepherd for whom, despite having conquered all six of the major peaks in the Cairngorms while still a young woman, the goal is not the mountaintop. 'One does not look upwards to spectacular peaks but downwards from the peaks to spectacular chasms,' she writes, for 'a mountain has an inside.' Shepherd walks 'into' rather than 'up' it. The mountain is her road to self-knowledge and, as she explores and comes to know its interior, she comes to know herself. There is little trace of her Presbyterian upbringing in the book, which is more Zen-like in its exploration of this connectedness between landscape and self. It is 'a journey into Being' which is described in language reminiscent of her poetry – as lyrical as it is sensual.

Interestingly, Shepherd's mountain is male, and gives itself most completely to her when she goes out merely 'to be with him'. It is almost as if the mountain is her lover, an observation which brings me rather neatly to another story in Shepherd's life, one which is surely guaranteed to satisfy the most prurient curiosity of biographers and readers alike.

Shepherd never married, but she did have a lover. At the end of her poetry anthology, *In the Cairngorms*, is a collection of eleven Petrarchan sonnets. Entitled 'Fourteen Years' they are, as

Ali Smith observes, 'bruised and oblique'. Whether the subject of these poems was Shepherd's fellow poet Charles Murray, or whether they were written, as has also been suggested, after the suicide of a married lover, is currently unknown. Furthermore, implicit in Shepherd's novels is the suggestion that emotional fulfilment exists beyond heterosexual union.

In attempting to solve these mysteries and write the stories in Shepherd's life, I had hoped to avoid too much footstepping. I thought I might find most of the answers to my questions through research carried out from the comfort of my study chair. Thanks to Google Maps, I have already 'walked' along North Deeside Road. I have even 'seen' the same view, from the sloping garden over the railway line to the River Dee, that Shepherd would have spied from her bedroom window.

A trip to Edinburgh is planned. There I have arranged to meet Erlend Clouston, Shepherd's literary executor, to sift through her private papers and spend some time exploring her archives at the National Library of Scotland and Scottish Poetry Library. I have even decided I might pop from Edinburgh to Aberdeen on an information-gathering exercise at the university library which holds letters to Shepherd from her closest friend, Agnes Mure Mackenzie. Perhaps I will be able to deduce from these whether those literary hints about sexual ambiguity have any foundation whatsoever.

From all these sources, I was sure I would be able to construct an authentic image of Nan Shepherd. And of course, there is also her writing. But despite Virginia Woolf's assurance that 'every secret of a writer's soul, every experience of his life, every quality of his mind is written large in his works,' the essence of Nan Shepherd continues to evade me. Even to her closest friends she was enigmatic. 'She was elusive. Reticent about herself. I began to know her essence by instinct,' Jessie Kesson said.

One of her former students described Shepherd as always seeming far way, somewhere else. Where? I think I knew the answer long before I came across some correspondence to Shepherd from her longstanding friend, the novelist Neil Gunn. In his last letter to her before his death in 1973 he wrote, 'You're like a lovely day in the hills.' It makes sense then, that that is where I will find Nan Shepherd. My road to knowledge is the Cairngorms, for it is where, as she says, 'I am'.

I have never climbed a mountain. Nor have I ever had any desire to. But I have now reached one inescapable conclusion: that is exactly what I will have to do. I have equipped myself with a pair of boots, booked a beginner's course in mountaineering and then I'm off to the Cairngorms, the most treacherous mountain range in Britain. My only consolation is that for Shepherd, the goal was never the summit.

Charlotte Peacock, a freelance photographer, took herself and her cameras to the Cairngorms this summer. As well as a biography of Nan Shepherd, she is currently working on a biografiction about Edward Thomas's women, and a novel: *Sparrow Fall*. In her spare time she raises her two daughters.

LAUREN RAZAVI

In Revolution

One night at a train station in Egypt

THE TOURIST POLICE ARRIVE AN HOUR AFTER THE INCIDENT.
By now, the train platform has returned to the animated calm that I've come to recognise as characteristic of Egypt at night. A bored child tugs at his mother's hijab, pressing his knuckles into tired eyes. Two men sit laughing outside one of the station cafés, sucking up tiny glasses of Arabic coffee in single gulps.

The four policemen stroll over to us. Tonight I've learnt that the tourist police have different responsibilities from the normal Egyptian police – primarily, to keep tourists out of troublesome situations while they're travelling in the country.

'We recommend that you vacate the area for your own safety please,' one officer says in monotone English. It's a line I imagine he practises in front of the mirror every morning.

I look at them blankly, too exhausted to articulate a reply, and my eyes flicker towards Mohammed. He speaks briefly with them in Arabic and they move down the platform, stopping to offer their advice to a trio of backpackers slouched against a crumbling wall.

'It's not good,' Mohammed says. 'Since the revolution... it's not good.'

I nod silently, and we continue to wait for the sleeper train, now five hours late.

IN REVOLUTION

*

My mother had begged me not to go. Footage and commentary on the *BBC News at Six* had told her everything she needed to know: that Egypt was no place for her 20-year-old daughter.

'Why can't you go to Italy or Spain?' she asked me three days before I left.

'Because I've been offered the chance to go to Egypt, Mum. And it's somewhere I've always wanted to go.'

She sighed. 'Why now? Why not give it a year or two for things to settle down a bit?'

I glanced at my father, hoping for a supportive comment. He was staring at his dinner plate, busying himself with arranging and rearranging his spaghetti bolognese.

'I'm going, Mum.'

She shook her head, the action soundtracked by sighs and grunts, and turned to my father. 'Mohsen, can you please *speak* to your daughter?'

He finally looked up, his eyes measuring us each for a moment before he spoke. 'Lynney, you know as well as I do, that once she's got an idea in her head, there'll be no stopping her.'

We finished the meal in silence. Later, my father told me he'd drive me to the airport, and slipped me £250 cash 'in case you run into trouble.'

*

I'd been travelling in Egypt for two weeks when we decided to take a train back to Cairo. I'd had only two jetlag-ridden days in the Egyptian capital when I first arrived, and I was keen to get back there and explore.

I'd spent most of my time so far drifting down the River Nile on a felucca, a traditional Egyptian sailboat, stopping to explore ancient temples and tombs along the way. The voyage had given me ample time to get to know Mohammed, the twenty-something tour guide who'd quickly become a friend.

So far, all the other transport had been in air-conditioned minibuses – complete with their own television sets and WiFi connections. I wasn't coping well with Egypt's over-the-top tourism amenities. They were stifling and disorienting. I wanted authenticity. I wanted to do things the local way. I told Mohammed this.

By the time we arrived in the market city of Aswan, we'd journeyed more than 500 miles south of Cairo. Aswan was Mohammed's hometown, and he spoke with wide eyes about its plethora of possibilities.

On our first evening in the city, we had set off together and lost ourselves in the hum of the streets. Market vendors and childhood friends stopped to say hello, and soon we were with a group of university students, talking politics and smoking shisha in a rickety street café.

It was April 2012 and it had been over a year since the Lotus Revolution ousted President Mubarak and ended his three-decade rule. The following month would see the first free presidential elections in the country's history. The future of the nation seemed to be at the forefront of everybody's mind, and each new person I met wanted to talk about it.

Hours later, the group had disbanded, and we were left inhaling an apple-flavoured shisha pipe. The conversation steadily turned from political matters to planning our route back to Cairo, and Mohammed suggested taking a sleeper train.

The trains were 'modern' and 'comfortable', and popular with locals because they were cheaper than flying, he explained. It would take twelve hours. Meals and coffee were included. There were smoking areas. Sleeper cabins held two people and had everything you could possibly need inside: beds, a sink and a window.

We booked the tickets. I saw it as a much better option than another minibus full of sunburnt middle-aged Westerners. Plus it sounded like an adventure.

*

Above the smog of the city was an oversized yellow moon. It was close enough tonight to make out the dark grooves and imperfections on its surface.

IN REVOLUTION

Mohammed and I had set off early in case traffic was bad on the way, but ended up arriving forty minutes before the train was due.

The station was lit with a scattering of cafés, their tables creeping out towards the tracks. We drank tea and chatted about Cairo and London.

Forty minutes passed, and the platform became busier and more animated. An hour passed. Then two hours. Soon, we stopped keeping track. Nobody had any information. Everybody was waiting. People shuffled about restlessly and drank tea and coffee they didn't want. I began to lose faith the train would ever arrive.

Out of nowhere, a howl shot down the platform. Rising male voices followed it. The old woman who'd shrieked shrunk down on her knees, wailing and whispering intermittently. What seemed to be a disagreement between two men had turned physical. They tugged on each other, nails digging into necks, and shirts ripping in the struggle. I felt the beat of my pulse echo in my ears.

Two more men approached, circling the commotion like lions. They tried to stop the fight, but quickly became involved themselves. Another two men stepped forward, then another three. The growing knot of men seemed to shudder; sides were taken, punches were thrown, and things escalated further.

Throngs of Egyptian men – from teenagers through to the elderly – joined the ruckus, palms in the air and bodies sprawling on the ground. I couldn't tell which limbs matched which faces. The handful of women I could see were standing back, shouting their pleas and protests between gasps.

One man grabbed a wooden chair and hurled it into the fray. My whole body tightened as it narrowly missed the head of a scrawny teenage boy. The café customers shrunk away or got involved. A proprietor ran out of his café carrying a crowbar and smacked someone over the head with it.

Why not give it a year or two for things to settle down a bit?
Once she's got an idea in her head, there'll be no stopping her.

My parents' words reverberated around my brain, and for the first time since I'd arrived in Egypt, I wondered if I really should have gone to Italy or Spain.

'Come, move this way.'

Mohammed ushered me down the platform as the fight took the shape of a riot. Panic was rippling across his face. I stood and watched it all unfold; it's the only thing either of us could do, our exit blocked by the throbbing pack.

'Why are they fighting?' I asked.

Mohammed shook his head. 'Something about someone's sister.' He paused. 'Small problems have a way of becoming big problems in Egypt now.'

I considered this for a moment before responding. I thought about the fights I'd seen on Friday and Saturday nights outside pubs and nightclubs back home; how violence can emerge quickly from just a wrong look or a muttered sentence.

As the conflict continued, I noticed three men in police uniform were stood watching what was going on.

'Why aren't the police doing anything?'

Mohammed paused. 'Police corruption was why the protests started,' he explained. 'Now, after the revolution, they are punishing us for it.'

As we spoke, the commotion began to dissipate. It was forgotten as hastily as it started. The cafés reopened and the patrons brushed off their seats and returned to them. The men whose disagreement had fuelled the mini-riot were checking on the frail old woman who had first alerted us to the situation with a scream.

I had experienced, first-hand, what the media has been calling 'unrest'. Egypt really was 'in a state of flux'. There were everyday symptoms of the revolution on the streets now, and this train station episode was perhaps just a glimpse of the larger picture. The country's cracks were displayed for anyone to see. And, according to Mohammed, they were getting bigger. This was the other side of the revolution.

*

It's after 3am when the train finally creaks into the station.

Mohammed speaks to the conductor and then turns to explain – finally – why the train is late. It turns out an entire village came out onto the tracks further down the line, a peaceful protest to draw the government's attention to their living conditions. The reaction to this news is muted. People don't appear surprised; this kind of disruption has become commonplace in post-revolution Egypt.

I want to ask more about the situation, but I look at Mohammed and decide he probably doesn't want to talk about it further. His eyes tell me he suffers the weight of his altered nation as much as he's excited by its new potential. I wonder how long he'll stay in Egypt, and whether it would be easy for him to leave if he wanted to.

We board the train and begin the journey back towards Cairo.

Lauren Razavi is a British-Iranian journalist whose work has been published in *The Guardian*, *The Times* and *The Washington Post* amongst other titles. She writes both fiction and non-fiction with a focus on people and cultures. She is currently working on her first book-length project, a family memoir-meets-travelogue about her childhood, her father and Iran.

BRIDGET READ

Dream-Work

A Confusion of Jacksons

I ONCE HAD A DREAM THAT MY DOG RAN FROM THE SECOND FLOOR OF OUR HOUSE and down the front stairs, straight out the open door onto the street. My sister and I chased after him until we found him in the park, where he had begun to grow a small, black Afro. He was playing with other dogs that all had human hair, as if they were wearing wigs, though we knew that they weren't.

We brought him back to our house and put him in my mother's big white bathtub. We pulled the showerhead out from its cradle at the end of the tub and began to wash him. As we did, our dog became a young Michael Jackson, maybe ten years old, looking like he does in the footage of The Jackson Five singing *I Want You Back* on *The Ed Sullivan Show*. He told us he had to get ready for tennis camp. My mother came upstairs with his mail, and handed him a letter. After a moment, he handed it back to her, and said, 'This isn't mine.' He pointed to the address on the front of the envelope: 'See, this is for *Samuel L* Jackson.' We apologized, but he was gracious. 'It happens all the time.'

Julia's Breakfast Shift

In my friend Julia's dream, the restaurant where she works is located inside her parents' house. She walks down the stairs from the first floor to the basement where the kitchen usually is, and there are the maroon leather banquettes with their fogged glass screens, and the tall bar against the wall filled with bottles and glasses, lit up from the back. Julia begins her breakfast shift, standing at the host's podium at the front of the restaurant, her parents' basement, and I am with her.

Paul walks in and asks for a table for two. Julia is surprised but I don't react, so she asks him to follow her and seats him politely at a table in the corner. When she returns to the podium, she looks at me, confused, so I say, to explain, 'He does that sometimes, and waits for me to sit with him.' I don't move from the podium. Julia watches as a waiter goes over to Paul to take his order, and that's where the dream ends.

The Oncologist Appears Older Than He Really Is

Paul told me that he dreamt that the doctor sitting on the end of his hospital bed was an old man. At least he felt like he was dreaming, even though he was still sitting up, propped against the pillows, listening to the doctor speak. He was middle-aged, balding, with a dark beard and a round face. But Paul saw him as an old, old man, with deep wrinkles in his neck and his hands, and white hair. It only lasted for a few seconds. Then the doctor was himself again.

He Was Glued To The Spot

Freud had a dream that he was walking up a set of stairs three at a time, delighted at his own agility. In the dream, a maid suddenly appears, walking down the opposite way, and Freud is embarrassed because he is not completely dressed. He tries to hurry away, ashamed, but finds he cannot move his feet.

*

I woke up with my mother and my sister and my aunt standing over me and it felt like a dream. I opened my eyes and found their heads and faces gathered above, like the fingers of a hand cupped around something sitting in its palm. The perspective was almost like one you might find in a sports movie, when someone has been hurt and is lying on the ground, and the camera films from their point of view as they regain consciousness. But these figures didn't swim in, dreamily – they were simply there, starkly, poised with too much urgency for it to be morning. I knew immediately that they would tell me Paul was dying, or dead.

When her father was dying of dementia, the writer Anne Carson dreamed an old recurring dream she had had as a child, in which she wakes up on the second floor of her house. She walks down the stairs to the living room, where she observes the dark green furniture and pale green walls. It is the same living room from her childhood home, but as an adult she felt upon waking that she had encountered some place completely different, as if the room had gone mad. It didn't scare her; she was consoled. She felt that the dream could save her, if only she could remember it.

Sigmund Freud said dreams were made up of two kinds of meanings, the latent and the manifest. The manifest dream is the dream itself as you wake up and recall it – Michael Jackson's hair on your dog, or the shiny marble floors of a restaurant in your family kitchen. These elements are only as important as the latent dream they disguise.

The latent dream is a product of the suppressed wishes of the unconscious mind that cannot be expressed in waking life, and so are transformed through what Freud called dream-work. In analyzing his dream with the maid on the stairs of his house, he attributed its manifest content to anxieties surrounding his health (damaged by his smoking), an argument he'd had with a maidservant at a patient's home (he had once spit on the staircase), and his attraction to women (although the maid in the dream was not beautiful).

Scientists in Kyoto have built something that they call a dream-reading machine. They gathered hundreds of reports on the brain activity of volunteers in the first stage of sleep, when a person is just entering drowsiness. As brain activity levels spiked, showing signs of hallucinations during slumber, researchers woke the volunteers and asked them to describe what they saw. Once these images were divided into categories like 'implements,' 'trees,' and 'people,' the scientists created a computer program that correlates specific brain activity in the visual cortex with images in a dream. With this data, they were able to predict what volunteers saw during sleep with 60% accuracy.

Technically, these are not the long, narrative visions that we truly think of as dreams, which occur during REM sleep, but researchers think the technique could potentially be applied to that stage in the future. 'Up until this moment, there were no grounds on which to say we don't just make up our dreams when we wake,' one of them said, and I suppose it's true.

A doctor named David Maurice thinks that humans experience REM sleep only to oxygenate our corneas. When we sleep with our eyes closed, the aqueous humor that sits in the anterior chamber just behind the cornea needs to be 'stirred' by brain activity, so we dream in order to bring much-needed oxygen to the most important part of the eye. He developed this line of inquiry after hearing about the case of a young man whose eyes had been paralyzed by an accident and left permanently open. His corneas had become laced with blood vessels.

Francis Crick and Graeme Mitchison wrote in 1983 that dreaming is merely a way for the brain to clear out excess cognitive debris, since our neural memory systems are not of infinite capacity: 'There is no evidence to suggest that remembered dreams are anything more than an accidental by-product of this function.'

*

When I dream about Paul, I know that he is dead. Is it not that the dreams are recreations of a time before his illness, or as if it had never happened. I'm not happy in them, usually. I am often crying. The first time, he said, 'It's OK,' over and over again, and I can remember nothing else. In another, he told me to stop crying, harshly. 'You can't do that.'

Last week I dreamt we were sitting on a beach. In the dream, the sand is grainy, like the red and brown pebbly kind you find on the Eastern Shore or Cape Cod. Unlike these places, the water at this beach is absolutely clear, so that we can see right down to the bottom. The tide is in, and we sit so that the sea comes just up to our chests. There are no waves. Paul holds me with my legs draped loosely over his, my arms around his neck, as if he is carrying me somewhere. 'I can't wait for the wedding,' I say, and that's it. He doesn't reply.

 The pleasure of dreaming is in the dissonance I feel when I find Paul there. In the state of a dream, I don't know when I will encounter him, what he will say, or what he'll do, and this is like a drug. It is the only time in which he feels to be truly embodied, given life outside my desires and memories. A separate, thinking, breathing person, though I know this is impossible.

 When a dream is over, I have to recreate everything that I saw and felt in order to relive it, to remember and hold onto it when I am awake. By doing so, everything in the dream becomes part of my imagining. I know that anyone I met there came only from inside my head. But I can recall the feeling, the initial shock and delight of that ecstatic recognition, like stepping, suddenly, into sunshine. It is the sensation of having experienced a miracle.

 I wanted to see a medium, someone who believes they can communicate with the dead, because I don't. What I have is more like a secret desire to believe, a streak of mad thought that sometimes – upon waking from a dream – seems faintly sane. I started looking into mediums located nearby and who advertise on the Internet. When I found one who shares my name, I called and made an appointment. That her website was called Silver Skys somehow made her services seem more appealing, as if the world to which she was connected was so strange and powerful that, in it, correct spelling had no use. She said I couldn't bring anyone into the room with me, in case she began picking up that person's energy accidentally. She said it would cost thirty pounds.

 When the time came to visit the medium I couldn't go. I began visualizing the meeting, and panicked, picturing myself sitting down with someone who would then try to tell me that Paul was there with her, or there through her, that Paul was somehow in the room. I thought I would run away. I thought I would try to hit her, or shake her, or I might go back, again and again. I couldn't even call to cancel, because I didn't want to hear her voice. So, after, when she tried to reach me, I let the phone ring and ring and ring.

Bridget Read was born in Los Angeles, and has a BA in English (Creative Writing) from Wesleyan University. Her work has appeared in New York and in the inaugural issue of *Words & Women* (Norwich, UK). She is currently writing a biography of a 20th-century American academic and literary critic.

SUZANNA ROSE

The Forgotten Filly of Bletchley Park

ON 18TH DECEMBER 1941, JUST TEN DAYS AFTER THE JAPANESE NAVY ATTACK on Pearl Harbor in Hawaii, my mother Janet Rose entered through the heavily guarded gates of Bletchley Park in Buckinghamshire for the first time. Janet, with her dark shoulder-length hair swept back from her face in a fashionable wave, would have been smartly dressed on this her first day of employment at Station X. Was she nervous, or at least a little apprehensive about starting work in such an unusual environment? Or maybe she was more concerned about whether her carefully set hair would flop in the damp morning air. Through the fog that was prevalent that day she would have glimpsed a view of the house at the end of the drive – hardly an impressive sight. The building has variously been described as hideous, grotesque, ghastly, sprawling or grand; as Victorian, Georgian, mock-Tudor or just plain old; as a mansion, a pile, or country house. From the outside the place looked ordinary enough but the work going on inside and the innumerable outbuildings that had sprung up like mushrooms within the grounds were anything but ordinary. For this was the centre of Britain's wartime codebreaking activities, where the Nazi Enigma ciphers were broken, thus helping to reduce the war by at least two years.

Before they began work, new recruits at the Park were given a security talk in the main house, where they were informed of the top secret nature of their employment. They then had to sign the Official Secrets Act. Following on from this, they would be taken to their future place of work in one of the many huts or other requisitioned buildings in the locality. As Janet was recruited by Dillwyn (Dilly) Knox as a codebreaker, she was sent to Hut 6 where she completed her training under Helen Morris, who remained a lifelong friend. Work was carried out both during the day and night on an eight hour shift system, with a break of only thirty minutes half way through. After six days, the staff had one day off before beginning the next rota.

On entering the hut for the first time, Janet would have seen several rows of desks, each with what looked like bulky typewriters placed in front of the women who worked there. These were Enigma machines, used to decode the messages coming from the Abwehr, a German military intelligence organisation. The women's job was to transcribe the reels of taped messages as they came through on the Enigma, by arranging and rearranging the dots on the tape which represented the transposed letters. It was repetitive work, requiring great concentration. Every possible combination of letters had to be tried, and once complete the messages were passed through to Hut 3 next door via an interconnecting tunnel. From there the messages were translated and then all intelligence gathered was sent to the relevant sections at Whitehall via motorbike courier. Direct contact with others in different sections was not encouraged. Work was carried out on a strictly 'need to know' basis in order to maintain the secrecy of operations taking place at the Park. One codebreaker, Oliver Lawn, no doubt reflected Janet's attitude at the time: 'The content of the messages was of no concern to me at all. I knew enough German to get an idea of what it was all about. But I had no idea of the context.'

Most Bletchley workers lodged in nearby towns and villages, and were transported to and from the site by shuttle bus. Until she found a room locally, Janet stayed with Helen Morris and her husband Christopher, who also worked at the Park as a cryptanalyst in the naval section. Janet later lodged in a council house, an experience she did not enjoy. Billeted conditions were basic, often with no bathroom and only an outside toilet. Some host families resented this unwelcome intrusion into their homes and the misconception that many of the civilians were conscientious objectors and only working at Bletchley in order to get out of enlisting, did not help matters. As they were unable to explain to anyone the contribution they were actually making to the war effort, this must have been quite awkward for the Bletchley workers.

Conditions in the huts were no better than in lodgings. The temporary buildings were overcrowded and cramped – freezing cold in winter and unbearably hot in summer. The windows were permanently blacked out, so the staff had to work under artificial light at all times. Toilets were in short supply, even after the new blocks were built in 1942. Frank Birch, in charge of the naval section in Block A, made a complaint about this to the works manager: 'There is only one [lavatory] for men and one for all the women, which is not enough for the 200 authorised.' Meals were taken at first in the main house and later in a purpose-built cafeteria. The food was generally considered awful, with one former employee commenting: 'Our canteen outshone any sleazy restaurant [...] One day I found a cooked cockroach nestling in my meat.'

Dilly had interviewed Janet in the front room of her digs in Great Missenden, where she was staying to be near to her husband, Victor, who was posted at barracks nearby. She said that it was the most extraordinary experience – more like a polite conversation with a family friend over a cup of tea than a formal discussion. The aim was obviously to put her at ease and tease out any likely problems. There must have been some concern about the time she spent in Munich with her German boyfriend before the start of war, but she evidently passed the test for she was engaged as a codebreaker on the spot. This was unusual, as most potential candidates had to have at least two interviews before they were taken on. Many of the staff were recruited through informal networks in the Services, universities and professions. However, this was not the case for Janet as she had not gone to university, neither was she part of the aristocracy nor a member of the Services. She was one of the many 'geese' who 'seem simply to have happened on it. Ignorant of the machinations of recruiters, they "somehow or by chance" came to work at BP.'

Boffins, as the mathematicians like Dilly were called, were known for their eccentricity and absent-mindedness.

THE FORGOTTEN FILLY OF BLETCHLEY PARK

They would wander around the premises in scruffy clothes or sometimes even in pyjamas and dressing-gown, much to the disapproval of one WAAF Officer, who describes 'filthy civilians with their greasy hair and dirty trousers.' What he lacked in appearance, however, Dilly certainly made up for in the way he treated his staff. He was very good to them, especially the women, and sometimes would take them out for the best meal available in the Seven Bells public house nearby. This group of women came to be known as 'Dilly's Fillies' and were all 'pretty girls.'

Sixty-five years after Janet left Bletchley Park, I went on a trip there to see for myself the place where she had worked. On arrival, we listened to a talk by a former MI6 officer, who then took our party on a tour round the buildings, explaining the nature of the work that took place on the site during the 1940s. I stopped off to take a closer look at Hut 6, where Janet was based. It seemed such an insignificant building, considering all that was achieved there and it was hard to imagine that this was the hub of Bletchley Park activities during the war.

While viewing the display of photographs in the main house, I stopped short in front of a rare picture supposedly of staff working inside Hut 6. I felt sure that one of the women sitting at a desk to the right of the room was Janet. Her profile was unmistakable, with her high cheekbones, wide forehead and hair swept away from her face. I photographed the display so that I could compare the image with a portrait I had of Janet that was done at a similar time. I was intrigued so, on my return home, I began to research Janet's past. I wished that I had paid more attention to her on the rare occasions when she talked about her wartime experiences. Of course, she was sworn to secrecy about her work at Station X. It wasn't until the thirty year rule was lifted in 1974 and the first book was published about the Ultra machine that details of the wartime work at Bletchley Park gained publicity. Most of the staff there had kept quiet about their role even to their closest family, and it is because of this that they have been referred to as Churchill's geese that laid the golden egg and never cackled.

By the time the film *Enigma* was released in 2001 most surviving Bletchley workers felt they were at last able to talk about their wartime role at Station X. I took Janet to see the film, feeling sure that she would be enthralled by it. However, glancing at her in the cinema I was surprised to find her frowning. Afterwards she complained that the portrayal of Bletchley on screen did not match up to her memories at all. Apart from anything else, the set was all wrong, as the filming had not taken place at Bletchley Park, but at Chicheley Hall nearby. Also, when Janet first arrived at the Park, there were about 2,000 people working there. Her section was 'a very small department' and she would have had little awareness of the affairs of others on site. Having recently watched the film again, I quite understand why Janet found it disappointing. This fictional story of adventure and romance would have born little resemblance to her experience at Bletchley. Newly married and with a strong Protestant work ethic, nothing would have been further from her mind than the thought of someone betraying their country.

Having discovered that all staff records at Bletchley Park were destroyed after the war, and that the Trust relies on friends and relatives to contact them with any information they might have about people who worked there, I set about gathering evidence of Janet's involvement at Station X. My first task was to locate a reference letter written by Janet's boss there that my sister had found amongst her papers after she died. This was written by P F G Twinn, who had taken over from Dilly Knox after his death in 1943, and confirmed Janet's employment at Bletchley from mid-December 1941 until the end of July 1942, when she became pregnant with my brother. Twinn describes Janet as being 'reliable and energetic' and states that she 'possesses in particular high qualities of intelligence and enterprise.' On the letter Janet had made a note about the *Codebreakers* book by Hinsley and Stripp, published in 1994. After locating her copy I found further notes written by her that included 'see after page 137 for my photo.' Sure enough, turning to the relevant page, I found the same photograph I had seen on display at Bletchley. An arrow with the name 'Janet' points towards the woman sitting on the right.

With the Twinn letter and the photograph confirming Janet's presence at Station X, I felt I had enough evidence to support having her name added to the list of employees at Bletchley Park.

THE FORGOTTEN FILLY OF BLETCHLEY PARK

With these, I recently contacted the Bletchley Park Trust via their website. As a result, Janet's name has now been added to the Roll of Honour, and with this came a certificate recognising her service in support of the work of Bletchley Park during World War II. It is heartening to know that this particular filly is no longer forgotten.

Suzanna Rose has spent most of her life in Suffolk. Her varied career includes working as cook, librarian, shopkeeper and information specialist. Having now retired from paid employment, Suzanna plans to concentrate on writing, especially about her adventures when travelling overland on the hippy trail to Kathmandu in the 1970s.

PHYLLIDA SCRIVENS

Not Without Risk

The story of an unlikely friendship, based on the unpublished memoirs of Leslie Linsay

ON THE NIGHT OF 20TH SEPTEMBER 1944, visibility on the Belgian-Dutch border was poor. Darkness combined with pungent swirling fog and the stench of sulphur; blood and urine fermenting with damp and sweaty khaki. Allied troops were tasked with manoeuvring their tanks over the already secured Meuse-Escaut canal, occupying the wooded marshy ground beyond and regaining the Belgian town of Hamont. At 0300 hours the exhausted soldiers of the East Yorkshires were relieved by the 1st Battalion of the Royal Suffolk Regiment under the command of Lieutenant Colonel Richard Walter Craddock.

First to approach the bridge was the Commander's jeep, bouncing precariously over the heavily pitted ground, cracked and crumbling after last evening's incessant heavy bombardment from Allied twenty five-pounders, each blast bright enough to permeate even closed eyelids. Mercifully, tonight the guns were silenced. Craddock and his batman were driven by Private Leslie Linsay. Just turned twenty, German-born Leslie was still getting used to his anglicised name, given by the Army just before his deployment to Europe a month earlier. His role was far more specific than that of the average Tommy. Leslie was the Interpreter, fluent in both German and Dutch.

NOT WITHOUT RISK

As the tyres rumbled off the bridge, fog amplified nearby enemy voices. Leslie instinctively focused; they were planning a counterattack. After rapidly radioing Brigade Headquarters, they were ordered to continue to Hamont, entering the main street at 0600 hours. Despite the good deal of shooting and a steady stream of prisoners, and due in part to the information supplied by Leslie, Hamont was designated as little more than a skirmish. But a few German soldiers had lost their lives and sadly two of Leslie's comrades were killed by shellfire. At first light, the townspeople emerged with Allied colours to drape from windows and brightly coloured flowers and ribbons to adorn the tanks. Jubilant crowds waved and wept, showering Leslie and his comrades with gifts of peaches, apples, wine and gratitude.

Eight months later the War in Europe was over and Leslie's battalion was billeted in the Hanover town of Enger. Following receipt of a letter from the Red Cross, Leslie borrowed a jeep and drove the one hundred and fifty miles to his family home in Hamburg, now in the occupied British Zone. It was his first return visit since boarding the Kindertransport for England in May 1939. Whatever horrors Leslie had experienced in ten months of combat, nothing could have prepared the young man for arrival in his childhood city.

Negotiating the potholes, he would have encountered convoys of celebrating Allied troops, but he had little reason to share their jubilation. For over a year Hamburg had resembled a scene from Hell. The skyline of this once magnificent medieval port was now a forest of hollow skeletal buildings, the soul sucked from them, the ground littered with piles of rocks, bricks and twisted metal. Coils of barbed wire, sandbags spilling into pools of stagnant water, decaying putrid rubbish, abandoned bicycles and burnt-out vehicles. And, most painful of all, queues of displaced people, their dead-fish eyes betraying exhaustion and disbelief as they waited silently for bread. During the summer of 1943, Operation Gomorrah, a joint British-American firebombing campaign, had reduced sixty per cent of the city to the contents of an incinerator along with 40,000 of its citizens.

Drawing closer to his home suburb of Rotherbaum, Leslie's mood may have lifted. The villas of this select residential area appeared to be intact. Driving down the elegant Neuer Jungfernsteig alongside the Alster Lake, he may have recalled his Jewish childhood, when, as Leopold Lievendag, affectionately known as Werner, he regularly enjoyed the sailboats and canoes on the gently lapping water.

'About 1880, as a young man, my paternal grandfather was unable to find work in his native Holland. He settled in Hamburg and being an extremely good shoemaker he prospered. Nearly half of his large family followed him to what was regarded as a haven.'

Drawing up at his old apartment at Halleplatz 8, Leslie was relieved to find his home of eight years still standing. The Red Cross letter had made it plain that Mutti and Papa would not be there. One November day in 1941 Samuel and Clara were deported to the Minsk Ghetto in Russia, joining 80,000 other Jews and dissenters. They would die there in the most appalling conditions. On entering the building, Leslie was confronted by a couple, once Nazi Party members, who were given possession of the apartment and all its contents after the previous occupants left. They nervously allowed the young British soldier to look around. His heart breaking, he was horrified to find no trace of his father's many canvases. Samuel Lievendag had been an accomplished artist, making a good living before the Nazi regime had stripped him of his livelihood. After knocking on many doors, Leslie found just one pen and ink drawing of the Hamburg Waterfront in the apartment of a particularly unpleasant character. When confronted, the man swore he was looking after it on behalf of the rightful owners. Leslie walked away clutching this precious memento of his past.

There was one more visit to make in Rotherbaum. On approaching the nearby villa belonging to his old friends the Sprenger family, Leslie could see people gathered inside. He was now taller and more mature than when he had escaped Nazi Germany as a fourteen year old. Would Herbert recognise him? He may well have straightened his army beret before standing to attention and knocking assertively. The door opened and a stranger informed him that Herr Sprenger had joined the *Wehrmacht* at the start of the war and been killed in action at Hamont in Belgium during September 1944. Surely not Hamont? Leslie did not wait to face Frau Sprenger. He had killed her husband! Driving away past the tennis club in Hallestrasse, his thoughts would have turned to how he first met Herbert Sprenger.

*

During the stifling summer heat of 1938 the privileged elite of Hamburg were more interested in tennis than politics. Am Rotherbaum Tennis Club was considered by many to be as prestigious as The All England Club in London. This was the home of the German Open, won the previous year by national hero Henner Henkel. The precisely raked clay courts resounded to the thump of tennis balls and polite applause from society spectators. Uniformed officers of the SS shared bottles of Rudesheimer with pretty Frauleins in wide-brimmed hats while the Nazi flag rippled proudly over the clubhouse. At thirty, popular club member Herbert Sprenger was enjoying a comfortable life with his wife and young family, paid for by his thriving floristry business. He could afford the exorbitant club fees and, while staff looked after the shop, Herbert indulged in a few sets almost every day. That summer the courts were fully booked from early morning to dusk, but there weren't enough ball boys to go round.

'By 1938 all restaurants, sports clubs, etc., displayed notices saying "Dogs and Jews Not Wanted". Some of my father's clients refused to pay him and he was unable legally to recover his debts owed by Aryan citizens.'

Under the unremitting strain, both Werner's parents fell ill, unable to earn enough money to pay the rent or even buy food. At fourteen he would have to find paid employment. The Tennis Club secretary didn't ask if he was a Jew so he didn't mention it. The other ball boys seemed to be there only to make enough pfennigs for cigarettes. Club members quickly learned that Werner was reliable. Herbert Sprenger admired the boy's conscientiousness and started asking for him by name, rewarding him with generous tips. These, on top of his standard rates of pay from the club, meant that Samuel soon cleared his debts. But the other boys became jealous and, on discovering Werner was Jewish, club members stopped using him. Only Herbert remained loyal, even increasing his gratuities, until the club was forbidden to employ Werner any longer. Instead, Herbert gave him a bicycle and the chance to work for him after school, delivering bouquets and floral tributes. In addition, Frau Sprenger cooked a daily meal for the growing boy. Werner would have looked forward to his visits to the Sprenger home, this formative relationship helping to shape Werner's views on humanity. Here was a well-liked and respected Aryan showing rare kindness to a Jewish family. But not without risk. The penalties for fraternising with enemies of the Third Reich were increasingly severe, with deportation, public hangings and on-the-spot shootings becoming commonplace. Werner's father asked Herbert why he continued to help the family, especially when he knew the dangers. Herbert replied that it had nothing to do with religion or politics. He just acted as any decent person should do – particularly a German one.

On the night of 10th November 1938 over 1,000 synagogues and 7,500 Jewish businesses throughout Germany and Austria were systematically destroyed by marauding gangs, encouraged by the Nazi hierarchy. This defining event became known as Kristallnacht. Alongside the frenzy of violence, Gestapo officers forcibly arrested every Jewish man and boy over sixteen, sending them to concentration camps to face an uncertain future.

That evening, Werner was staying overnight with his elderly uncle and aunt in another part of the city. Setting off to school the following morning, he was alarmed and confused by the mounds of shattered glass littering the streets. At the Talmud Torah School, Gestapo officers were rounding up the male teachers and older boys. At fourteen Werner was spared and sent home. But his apartment was empty. He was again forced to negotiate the dangers of the streets, suffering beatings from Brown Shirts and others brandishing sticks and heavily buckled belts. Arriving back at his uncle's house the old man and young Werner were instantly arrested. Fortunately, a friend of his uncle, despite being a Party Member of very long standing, disagreed with this outrage and obtained their release. After three days in hiding, Samuel and Clara slipped back unnoticed into their apartment, having been secreted in the home of Christian friends, successfully evading Samuel's arrest. Despite the worsening situation, Herbert Sprenger continued to defy the authorities, even after Werner had left for England, secretly employing Samuel to design posters for his shop. That is, until the couple's deportation to Minsk.

*

In 1970, still struggling emotionally over the circumstances of Herbert's death, Leslie took his English wife Joan and eldest son David to Hamburg, looking for Frau Sprenger. The whole area had been rebuilt and the florist's shop gone. On the return journey through Belgium they visited Hamont, hoping to find Herbert's grave. He was not there. They asked at the local convent where the nuns suggested they enquire at the German War Cemetery in nearby Lommel.

The archivist proved most helpful, informing Leslie that Obergefreiter Sprenger had been killed on 8th September 1944 at the Battle of Hechtel, some twelve days before the Battle of Hamont. The two towns are separated by only thirteen miles and by the time the 1st Suffolks had entered Hamont, Herbert was already dead.

'For twenty-five years I suffered a guilt complex convinced I was instrumental in causing the death of a person to whom I owed nothing but gratitude. This destroyed almost everything in which I believed.'

Unlike the British, the German troops did not bury their battle dead and Herbert's body most probably remained where it fell until some days later when the Resistance would have taken the bodies for burial at Lommel, two soldiers to each grave. His conscience clear, Leslie could at last visit his friend and thank him for the kindness and compassion shown to his family. He may even have whispered the Mourner's Kaddish for Herbert's soul.

Leslie never did trace Frau Sprenger.

Phyllida Scrivens is fascinated by people's lives. Writing feature interviews for a Surrey newspaper proved invaluable preparation for her current major project: a full-length biography of a German boy who, having walked across Europe to escape the Nazis, took a Kindertransport to England and became Sheriff of Norwich.